AAT

TECHNICIAN

NVQ AND LEVEL 4 DIPLOMA FOR ACCOUNTING TECHNICIANS (QCF)

COMBINED **COMPANION** Unit 10

Managing Systems
and People in
the Accounting
Environment

LEARNING MEDIA

First edition 2004
Fourth edition May 2009

ISBN 9780 7517 6704 9 (previous edition 0 7517 2896 5)

British Library Cataloguing-in-Publication Data
A catalogue record for this book is available from the British Library

Published by

BPP Learning Media Ltd
BPP House
Aldine Place
London W12 8AA

www.bpp.com/learningmedia

Printed in the United Kingdom

Your learning materials, published by BPP Learning Media Ltd, are printed on paper sourced from sustainable, managed forests.

We are grateful to the AAT for permission to reproduce their case study.
The sample report has been prepared by BPP Learning Media Ltd.

CONTENTS

INTRODUCTION

This edition of BPP's Combined Companion for AAT Technician Unit 10, Managing Accounting Systems and People in the Accounting Environment has been carefully designed to enable students to practise all aspects of the requirements of the Standards of Competence and performance criteria, and to ultimately produce a successful project.

The chapters contain these key features:

- clear, step by step explanation of the topic

- clear guidance on how to produce a professional management report and an explanation of the key contents of one

- logical progression and linking from one chapter to the next

- practical guidance on completion of each section based on the organisation chosen

- Case Study advice at the end of each chapter for students completing this project with an AAT Case Study Scenario

- The AAT Sample case study and specimen report.

Tutors adopting our Companions (minimum of ten Course Companions and ten Revision Companions per Unit, or ten Combined Companions as appropriate) are entitled to free access to the Lecturers' Area resources. To obtain your log-in, e-mail lecturersvc@bpp.com.

Home Study students are also entitled to access to additional resources. You will have received your log-in details on registration.

If you have any comments about this book, please e-mail helendarch@bpp.com or write to Helen Darch, AAT Publishing Manager, BPP Learning Media Ltd, BPP House, Aldine Place, London W12 8AA.

Level 4 Diploma for Accounting Technicians

This Combined Companion is suitable for all students studying for Unit 10, whether for the NVQ or the Diploma Pathway.

UNIT 10 STANDARDS OF COMPETENCE

The structure of the Standards for Unit 10

The Unit commences with a statement of the knowledge and understanding which underpin competence in the Unit's elements.

The Unit of Competence is then divided into elements of competence describing activities which the individual should be able to perform.

Each element includes:

a) a set of performance criteria. This defines what constitutes competent performance.

b) a range statement. This defines the situations, contexts, methods etc in which competence should be displayed.

c) evidence requirements. These state that competence must be demonstrated consistently, over an appropriate time scale with evidence of performance being provided from the appropriate sources.

d) sources of evidence. In Unit 10, evidence requirements are closely linked to the assessment strategy. You are required to write a 4,000 word report based on an accounting system.

The elements of competence for Unit 10 *Managing Systems and People in an Accounting Environment* are set out below. Knowledge and understanding required for the unit as a whole are listed first, followed by the performance criteria and range statements for each element. Performance criteria are cross-referenced below to chapters in this Unit 10 *Managing Systems and People in an Accounting Environment* Combined Companion.

Unit 10 Managing Systems and People in the Accounting Environment

Unit Commentary

This Unit is about your role as a manager in the accounting environment, whether you are a line manager or are managing a particular function or project.

The first element requires you to show that you co-ordinate work activities effectively within the accounting environment. This includes setting realistic objectives, targets and deadlines and managing people in such a way that these can be met. You also need to show that you prepare contingency plans to cover a variety of problems that can reduce the likelihood of meeting objectives, targets and deadlines.

The second element is about identifying weaknesses in an accounting system and making recommendations to rectify these. This involves identifying potential for misuse of a system, whether this is accidental (errors) or deliberate (fraud). You are also required to update the system, for example to comply with legislative requirements, and to check that the output is correct after the system has been updated.

Elements contained within this unit are:

Element 10.1   Manage people within the accounting environment

Element 10.2   Identify opportunities for improving the effectiveness of an accounting system

Knowledge and understanding

To perform this unit effectively you will need to know and understand:

The Business Environment

1   The range of external regulations affecting accounting practice (Element 10.2)

2   Common types of fraud (Element 10.2)

3   The implications of fraud (Element 10.2)

Management Techniques

4   Methods for scheduling and planning work (Element 10.1)

5   Techniques for managing your own time effectively (Element 10.1)

6   Methods of measuring cost-effectiveness (Element 10.2)

7   Methods of detecting fraud within accounting systems (Element 10.2)

8   Techniques for influencing and negotiating with decision-makers and controllers of resources (Element 10.1)

9   Techniques for reviewing recommendations through cost-benefit analysis (Element 10.2)

Management Principles and Theory

10   Principles of supervision and delegation (Element 10.1)

11   Principles of fostering effective working relationships, building teams and motivating staff (Element 10.1)

The Organisation

12   How the accounting systems of an organisation are affected by its organisational structure, its Management Information Systems, its administrative systems and procedures and the nature of its business transactions (Elements 10.1 & 10.2)

13   The overview of the organisation's business and its critical external relationships (customers/clients, suppliers, etc.) (Elements 10.1 & 10.2)

14   The purpose, structure and organisation of the accounting function and its relationships with other functions within the organisation (Element 10.2)

15   Who controls the supply of resources (equipment, materials, information and people) within the organisation (Element 10.1)

Element 10.1 Co-ordinate work activities within the accounting environment

Performance criteria

In order to perform this element successfully you need to:

A   Plan work activities to make the optimum use of resources and to ensure that work is completed within agreed timescales

B   Review the competence of individuals undertaking work activities and arrange the necessary training

C   Prepare, in collaboration with management, contingency plans to meet possible emergencies

D   Communicate work methods and schedules to colleagues in ways that help them to understand what is expected of them

E   Monitor work activities sufficiently closely to ensure that quality standards are being met

F   Co-ordinate work activities effectively and in accordance with work plans and contingency plans

G   Encourage colleagues to report to you promptly any problems and queries that are beyond their authority or expertise to resolve, and resolve these where they are within your authority and expertise

H   Refer problems and queries to the appropriate person where resolution is beyond your authority or expertise

Range statement

Performance in this element relates to the following contexts:

Contingency plans allowing for:

- Fully functioning computer system not being available

- Staff absence

- Changes in work patterns and demands

Element 10.2 Identify opportunities for improving the effectiveness of an accounting system

Performance criteria

In order to perform this element successfully you need to:

A   Identify weaknesses and potential for improvements to the accounting system and consider their impact on the operation of the organisation

B   Identify potential areas of fraud arising from control avoidance within the accounting system and grade the risk

C   Review methods of operating regularly in respect of their cost – effectiveness, reliability and speed

D   Make recommendations to the appropriate person in a clear, easily understood format

E   Ensure recommendations are supported by a clear rationale which includes an explanation of any assumption made

F   Explain to those affected the implications of **recommended changes** in terms of financial costs and benefits

Range statement

Performance in this element relates to the following contexts:

Weaknesses:

■   Potential for errors
■   Exposure to possible fraud

Accounting system:

■   Manual
■   Computerised

Recommendations:

■   Oral
■   Written

Changes affecting systems:

■   External regulations
■   Organisational policies and procedures

ASSESSMENT STRATEGY

This Unit is assessed by means of a project plus assessor questioning and employer testimony.

The project takes the form of a report to management that analyses the management accounting system and the skills of the people working within it. It should identify how both might be enhanced to improve their effectiveness. In producing this report students will need to prove competence in the co-ordination of work activities and the identification and trading of fraud in that system. Students may be able to identify weaknesses and make recommendations for improvement. All changes made must be monitored and reviewed for their effectiveness.

The total length of the project (excluding appendices) should not exceed 4,000 words. An appropriate manager should attest to the originality, authenticity and quality of the project report. The project should be based on an actual management accounting system, or part-system, within the student's workplace in the present or recent past. For students not in relevant employment, an unpaid placement such as a voluntary organisation or charity, club or society or a college department may be suitable. Alternatively (if no work placement is available/the student is not in employment) an AAT simulation in the form of a case study should be used as the basis of the project.

The Approved Assessment Centre's role

The AAC should undertake the following steps:

- make an initial assessment of the project idea

- use one-to-one sessions to advise and support the student

- encourage workplace mentors to participate (testimony etc)

- ensure the project is the student's original work

- use formative assessments and action plans to guide the student

- undertake summative assessment against performance criteria, range statements and knowledge and understanding

- sign off each performance criterion

- conduct a final assessment interview with documented questioning

The student's role

The student should ensure that the project's format is such that it:

- covers all performance criteria, range statements and knowledge and understanding
- covers the objectives set out in the Terms of Reference of the project
- is well laid out, easy to read and includes an executive summary
- uses report form style with appropriate language
- shows clear progression from one idea to the next
- cross-refers the main text to any appendices
- uses diagrams and flow charts appropriately
- starts each section on a fresh page

Note

The simulation will place students in a simulated work place role play situation, where they will be given a range of tasks to undertake. The simulation will aim to cover as many of the performance criteria and as much of the underpinning knowledge and understanding as is considered to be feasible for the scenario.

Where all of the listed performance criteria and underpinning knowledge and understanding have **not** been addressed sufficiently by the simulation, documented assessor questioning **must** be employed to address any gaps.

All performance criteria and underpinning knowledge and understanding must be evidenced.

chapter 1:
THE BASIC PRINCIPLES OF UNIT 10

chapter coverage 📖

The basic principles of Unit 10:

✍ The management report

✍ NVQ students

✍ Diploma Pathway students

✍ Your organisation or the AAT Case study?

✍ FAQs

The Unit 10 Management Report

The Unit 10 project should be presented to your assessor as a report to management, with appropriate appendices. It must be written in a professional business style, and analyse four key areas of the organisation and make recommendations to improve them.

The four key areas of the organisation are:

1) the management of people
2) an accounting system (or part of one)
3) fraud – its risk and the controls in place
4) contingency planning

This report can either be based on the organisation where you work or on an AAT written Case Study that your assessor can provide you with.

NVQ students

As you are completing your qualification based on a portfolio of work-based evidence (or simulated work-based evidence) it will be expected that you complete this report on your work place. If you are unable to do this you should discuss this decision with your assessor before starting your work.

Diploma students

You can choose whether to write the report around your own organisation or the Case Study without needing to discuss this decision with your assessor.

The report should be between 3,500 and 4,500 words in length; however this is only a guide. You and your assessor should ensure that your work covers all of the standards required in this unit in order that it be assessed as competent.

If your work is significantly under this count then it probably does not contain all the areas required. Map it carefully to the standards (see Chapter 8) and ensure all are covered sufficiently.

If your finished report is much longer than this then it may be too wordy or you may have more in it than required. Ask your assessor for advice and ensure that your word count does *not* include your appendices.

The report must also be written in an appropriate format and include certain sections. The final version must include the following:

- Title Page
- Contents
- Executive Summary
- Introduction to the organisation
- Terms of Reference

- Methodology
- Management of People
- Analysis of an Accounting System
- Fraud Controls
- Contingency Planning
- Cost Benefit Analysis
- Appendices

This Companion will take you through the four key areas of the report and explain each in detail and how to achieve competence in them. It will also guide you through the compilation of the report and the other sections required to be in it and why.

It will then explain to you how to map your work to the standards and ensure all areas are covered. In each section it explains which standards must be covered and gives guidance and support on how to do this.

Once you are a fully qualified AAT Technician an employer would expect you to be able to produce a professional management report in an appropriate style and format. By the time you have completed this unit these are the skills and knowledge you will have gained.

Own organisation or Case Study?

Own organisation

If you work in an organisation where you can investigate the four key standard areas and report to management on them, then this is the best approach to take. This will not only mean you produce a good report that is competent but also that you have added value to your organisation and ensured your recommendations are noted by management.

You may be thinking that your organisation is too large or too controlled by management for any of your recommendations to be implemented but this does not matter. Implementation is not a requirement of this unit.

The main outcome of your work should be that you have investigated the 4 key areas and made recommendations for improvement. By having done this you will have gained a great deal of knowledge about your work place and this can only enhance your value to your organisation.

You may also be thinking that there are no improvements to be made, perhaps your workplace is already perfect! It is usual that after further research some improvements can be identified – again, we stress that they do not have to be implemented. If you complete your research and find that there are no recommendations to make then this is acceptable (though very rare!) As long as in your detailed report you have covered all the standards in sufficient detail then your work should be assessed as competent.

Note however, that in order to complete this work based on your work place you will require your manager's approval. They will need to sign an authenticity statement once you have presented them with your final report to testify that it is based on the work place and is a true representation of it. They will also be required to testify that the work is your own, unaided and that your recommendations have been discussed with them orally. You must have their approval to do this, as without this statement your assessor can not assess your work.

If, after consideration, you find that you are unable to investigate all 4 areas of the standards in your own organisation then you may find that the Case Study is for you. This is often the case for students who work in practice and so are dealing with clients and their accounts on a daily basis and not with the other areas, such as the management of people.

If this applies to you then the first step should be to discuss this with your manager at work. Some students have added value to a client by producing a report on their organisation (the client's name can be changed or omitted for confidentiality). After all, you will effectively become a management consultant while researching and compiling the report; this can be an extremely useful exercise if your company and the client is willing to allow you to do this.

It may be the case that your employer does not know you are studying or that you are not working in an accounting role and therefore you are not able to investigate and report on an accounting system. If this is the case then the AAT Case Study scenario may be more appropriate for you.

Case Study

If completing your work based on the Case Study you will need to ensure that it reads as if you work in the organisation according to the brief. Your final report should be no different to that of a student who is writing based on their own organisation.

You must read through the entire case study and assume all the information contained within it is your own knowledge of the work place. As you complete each section of your report you will write it assuming that your assessor has no prior knowledge of the organisation.

Your assessor will take the place of the work place manager and needs to produce an authenticity statement at the end once competence has been achieved. In order that they can do this, you will need to provide them with drafts of your work so that they can give advice, support and feedback but also be assured it is your own and unaided work. You must be in constant contact with them throughout the process.

Case Study Advice

This Companion features specific advice within each chapter on how to use the Case Study to complete your work. Look out for the paragraphs formatted like this.

The Unit 10 project for students for whom English is their second language

The AAT qualification is an English language-based qualification and to complete it you will be required to demonstrate an ability to write a professional report – in English. If English is not your first language this may prove difficult for you. There are several practical things you can do to support you in this:

1) Talk to your assessor – they will be able to advise and support you (but note they can not proof read or correct your work for you)

2) Ask a friend or colleague to be a mentor – they are able to proof read your work and advise you on any amendments that can be made

3) Turn on your spellchecker – the finished report needs to be typed so complete it on a word processing package with your spellchecker and grammar checker turned on to highlight any errors made

4) Contact your AAT members' society – they may be able to provide you with an AAT member volunteer who can proof read your work and advise you on the completion of it

Your assessor must be confident that your finished and final report is professional and in good business English. They can not report it as competent unless it is. If you need help and support to do this then raise this as early as possible in the process.

FAQs

1) **What areas must my project cover?** – The management of People, An Accounting System (or part of one), Fraud and Contingency Plans.

2) **Does this have to be based on my work place?** – No, the AAT produce a Case Study on which you may base your report but in this case it should look no different to a report based on a real organisation. To complete it you will have to assume you work in the organisation and all the information contained in the scenario is knowledge you have assuming you work there.

3) **How long should the finished report be?** – Approximately 4,000 words; however you must cover all the standards and lay the report out in a certain format so if you are significantly under or over this amount talk to your assessor for advice.

student notes

4) **Should I write the whole report then submit it for assessment?** – No. This is dangerous as your assessor must be sure your work is authentic and if you do this they will be unable to be sure. Also it is very difficult to produce a perfect report first time.

Submit a proposal and drafts to your assessor and get feedback and support as your complete your work. This will not only make the process easier for you but ensure they are comfortable that your work is your own.

5) **My English is not very good – will this affect my competence?** – It could do, yes. Your final report must be in English and be in a professional written style. See the section in this chapter on students for whom English is a second language for advice and support on how to ensure your work is to an acceptable standard.

6) **Must my project cover all the standards?** – Yes. In order to be judged competent you must cover all the standards sufficiently including the performance criteria, range statements and knowledge and understanding. See the chapters on the assessment process and mapping to assist you in doing this.

chapter 2:
THE UNIT 10 ASSESSMENT PROCESS AND STANDARDS

chapter coverage 📖

- ✍ Assessment standards

- ✍ Assessment process

- ✍ AAT Standards of Competence

- ✍ Frequently Asked Questions (FAQs)

Assessment standards

The Unit 10 project is assessed once completed by the student. As part of the assessment process the assessor is required to confirm that the work meets the following criteria (VACS):

- **V**alid – it meets the standards

- **A**uthentic – it is the student's own, unaided work

- **C**urrent – it has been written recently and reflects how the organisation currently operates

- **S**ufficient – it investigates the key areas in sufficient detail to meet the standards

Its **validity** is assured by the student mapping the work to the standards. This means that you must cross-reference all your work to the standards of this unit. To do this you must number all the pages and paragraphs of your work and write the relevant paragraph number into a mapping document next to the standards they refer to.

Authenticity is assured by the student and the assessor working together through the project. This process starts with the student submitting a proposal to the assessor, which the assessor feeds back on. Your assessor should then review drafts of your work as you progress and provide further feedback on this. This aids them in being sure your work is your own and unaided. It is worth also noting that they may not be able to authenticate work that is presented to them as a fully completed report where they have not seen and fed back on drafts as it is written.

For students completing this report on their work place they then require a signed and dated statement, on company headed paper, from their manager testifying that the work is their own, unaided and a true reflection of the work place. If this can not be obtained then the Case Study would be a better option for the student.

Case Study students have their assessor act as their manager. In these cases the assessor signs and dates a witness statement to the same effect as the work place manager above. It is even more critical that for Case Study reports the student submits drafts and the assessor feeds back on them.

Authenticity is also confirmed through a final interview between the student and the assessor once the work has been submitted and assessed. In the final interview the assessor asks the student questions about the work they have completed. This enables them to confirm the work is their own and unaided.

Currency is concerning whether the report is up-to-date and relevant in the work place. It is worth remembering this and ensuring your work is assessed as soon as possible after its completion. Many students start this project and then do not complete it for some time, possibly years, later. This may mean that their work is no longer current and so a new project would have to be written.

Sufficiency is related to the work covering the standards to sufficient detail for the assessor to be sure that it meets the standards required. A good example is within the contingency planning part of the report. The range statement for this standard (more on this later in this chapter) states that the report must cover absence of staff, loss of IT and changes in work patterns and demands. All three have to be covered, and in sufficient detail.

Extract from a student's project:

6.2 Staff Absence

6.2.1 If staff are absent from work in the long term then XYZ plc would plan to replace them with temporary staff recruited from an agency.

The plan above may well be true but it is not sufficient in terms of investigating the company's current plans.

For example:

- Where is a temp resourced from?
- Are there minimum skills, experience or qualifications required? Who recruits them?
- Who trains them?
- Is there a plan of the duties they will take on to leave more experienced staff completing the more demanding ones?
- Are there procedures so that they can pick up the work required of them quickly and who monitors their work and checks its quality?

You can imagine all these areas being important and of concern. If a key member of staff is absent then their work will need to be covered quickly so all these issues need to be addressed. The investigation into the plan, in order to be of sufficient detail, needs to address these factors.

A good test of whether a plan is working is also to investigate what happened when it is put into place. There is more on this in the contingency planning chapter of this Companion but this simple example sets the scene on what investigations are sufficient for the report.

Assessment process

The assessment process has already been discussed in this chapter but it is important that you, the student, understands it fully so that you can ensure you complete your work appropriately, get it assessed promptly and complete this unit and your Technician level.

The first stage of the process is that the assessor should discuss the project with you and review your initial ideas. This is a **project proposal** and can either be done through you submitting a formal written document or in a one

student notes

to one discussion with your assessor. Either way a documented record of this must be kept as it might be reviewed by the AAT once competence has been achieved.

The assessor will, at this stage, agree with you an **assessment plan**. This should cover how the report will be completed and in what timescales. It should include a plan as to when each draft will be submitted for feedback and when the final version will be ready.

The assessment plan is just that – a plan. It will then get revised and updated as the project progresses and again is a key part of the document audit trail required by the AAT for this unit.

Once the approach to the report has been agreed then **drafts** should be submitted to your assessor for review and feedback. This ensures that you keep on the right track as you complete the work and that the assessor can be sure your work is your own and unaided.

Do not complete too much of the report before submitting it. Any assessor might be suspicious of a fully completed report being handed in for assessment if they have not worked with and guided the student through its completion.

One of the requirements the AAT place on assessors is that they ensure you have **mapped your work to the required standards**. This is covered in detail in Chapter 8, for now it is important to understand that your work will not be accepted without this mapping. It must meet 100% of the standards in order that it can be assessed.

Once a **final version** of your report has been agreed then it must be **professionally presented** and submitted for assessment. It must be submitted with your **manager's authenticity statement** (if completing the report on your work place) and with your full mapping to the standards. It must include all the formatting requirements discussed later in this Companion and all the required sections, *each starting on a new page*.

The assessor then undertakes a **final assessment** of the work. They do this in a number of different ways and are, in essence, confirming the VACS criteria discussed earlier in this chapter. This is then documented and fed back to you.

The final stage of the assessment process for this unit then takes place once the assessor has assessed the work to the VACS criteria. This is a **final interview** and takes place between the student and the assessor to discuss the work, its completion and key outcomes.

The assessor can also use the final interview to ask questions regarding any areas of the standards that were weak in the final report. This gives them a small amount of flexibility in their assessment although it would not be expected that this be used to assess to sufficient detail the key areas of the report. It is used more to test and probe further a point and this aids them in confirming the authenticity of the work.

Then the assessor submits the work for **internal verification (IV)**. This is an internal quality assurance system required by all such qualifications. For the Diploma Pathway the name is slightly different, **internal quality assurance moderation (IQAM)**, but the principle is the same.

The centre IV/IQAM checks a sample of all assessors work in order that they can check it is to standard and provide appropriate feedback and support. Although it would not be expected that the assessor's decision of competence be overturned as a result of this, it could happen and you could be asked to amend your work or update it.

Once your finished project (portfolio for NVQ route) has passed this check it is then **reported to the AAT**.

NVQ students

Your result will then be updated by the AAT and you will show as competent in this unit. The AAT then may call your project in as a sample from your college for scrutiny by an AAT expert. They will review your work and the assessment audit trail and, if required, they will make recommendations to the assessor and college on how to improve the overall assessment of Unit 10.

They may, on occasion, overturn an assessment decision though this is extremely rare.

Diploma students

Your result will then be updated by the AAT as a provisional result. For the Diploma Pathway a sample of assessed units are requested for submission to the AAT within a number weeks of the competence being reported. If this is the case your work will again be scrutinised and advice and support provided to your assessor and college.

Again, it is rare that the overall assessment decision be overturned but this does, on occasion, occur. If this is the case your assessor will contact you with information about the additional work required for competence.

Once this period has passed, or your work is scrutinised and accepted, your provisional result will then be updated.

student notes

11

student notes ✍

The assessment process

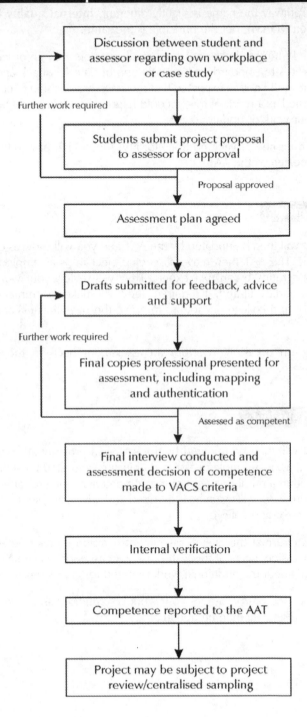

Discussion between student and assessor regarding own workplace or case study

Further work required

Students submit project proposal to assessor for approval

Proposal approved

Assessment plan agreed

Drafts submitted for feedback, advice and support

Further work required

Final copies professional presented for assessment, including mapping and authentication

Assessed as competent

Final interview conducted and assessment decision of competence made to VACS criteria

Internal verification

Competence reported to the AAT

Project may be subject to project review/centralised sampling

The AAT Standards of Competence

The AAT Standards of Competence (or syllabus) are the areas that you have to show competence in, in order to demonstrate that you can perform the duties and tasks required.

To complete a unit successfully you must demonstrate competence in all of the Standards of Competence.

The Standards are broken down into 3 levels – **elements**, **performance criteria** and **range statements**. These are then also supported by what is called **knowledge and understanding**. It is not enough that you can demonstrate the correct accounting treatment for bad debts, for example, but that the assessor must also ensure that you understand why this is the case.

Elements

The elements to a unit break it down into broad sections where competence must be demonstrated.

> **To clarify with an example**:
>
> Imagine you are undertaking an NVQ in cake baking.
>
> First of all the standards for this might be broken down into elements such as:
>
> - Buying and preparing the ingredients
> - Mixing the ingredients and preparing
> - Cooking the cake
>
> These split the overall unit out into the stages require to complete the process.

The Unit 10 standards have 2 elements:

10.1 Co-ordinate work activities within the accounting environment.

10.2 Identify opportunities for improving the effectiveness of an accounting system.

Performance Criteria

The performance criteria then break the elements down further into more detailed requirements to demonstrate competence.

> **Taking the cake baking example:**
>
> The first element – buying and preparing the ingredients – may then include performance criteria such as:
>
> - purchasing ingredients,
> - weighing solid ingredients
> - measuring out liquids
> - sieving flour

The Unit 10.1 element – *co-ordinate work activities within the accounting environment* includes (among many others) the example performance criteria below.

A   Plan work activities to make the optimum use of resources and to ensure that work is completed within agreed timescales.

C   Prepare, in collaboration with management, **contingency plans** to meet possible emergencies.

E   Monitor work activities sufficiently closely to ensure quality standards are being met.

Range statement

You will notice that above the words **'contingency plans'** are in bold type. This is because there is a range statement associated with them. The range statement shows you exactly what that certain area must cover.

> **Taking the cake baking example:**
>
> The performance criteria *'weighing ingredients'* may require you to demonstrate competence in both imperial and metric measures
>
> and under *'measuring liquids'* you may have to demonstrate that you can measure teaspoons, tablespoons etc.

Under **contingency planning** the Standards for Unit 10 have the following range statements:

Contingency plans for:

- Fully functioning computer system not being available
- Staff absence
- Changes in work patterns and demands

To be competent in this unit you will have to ensure your work covers all 3 aspects of this performance criteria, in sufficient detail.

Knowledge and understanding

This tests that you understand why particular performance criteria must be covered and the logic and reasoning for them.

> **Taking the cake baking example:**
>
> Do you know why flour must be sieved when making a cake?
>
> Which is the correct answer?:
>
> A: It is to incorporate air into the mixture and remove lumps
> B: Because you told me I have to
>
> A is obviously the correct answer. B does not demonstrate the knowledge and understanding required so does not achieve competence.

Examples of Knowledge and Understanding that must be demonstrated by the Unit 10 project include:

4   Methods for scheduling and planning work

5   Techniques for managing your own time effectively

6   Methods of measuring cost effectiveness

7   Methods of detecting fraud within accounting systems

8   Techniques for influencing and negotiating with decision-makers and controllers of resources

9   Techniques for reviewing recommendations through cost benefit analysis

The full set of standards for Unit 10 and where they are addressed by this Companion are listed below. At the beginning of each chapter we also provide information on the standards that a particular chapter covers.

Be warned however, – your report must not be a list of paragraphs that addresses each of these in turn. It must follow the prescribed format included in this Companion and if it does appear as a list your assessor will ask you to adjust your work to the appropriate style.

student notes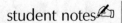

Standards of competence
Element 10.1
A   Plan work activities to make the optimum use of resources and to ensure that work is completed within agreed timescales.
B   Review the competence of individuals undertaking work activities and arrange the necessary training.
C.   Prepare, in collaboration with management, **contingency plans** to meet possible emergencies.
D.   Communicate work methods and schedules to colleagues in ways that help them to understand what is expected of them.
E.   Monitor work activities sufficiently closely to ensure quality standards are being met.
F.   Co-ordinate work activities effectively and in accordance with work plans and contingency plans.
G.   Encourage colleagues to report to you promptly any problems and queries that are beyond their authority or expertise to resolve, and resolve these where they are within your authority and expertise.
H.   Refer problems and queries to the appropriate person where resolution is beyond your authority or expertise.
Range statement:
I.   Contingency plans allowing for: Fully functioning computer system not being available
Staff absence
Changes in work patterns and demands

Standards of competence
Element 10.2
A   Identify weaknesses and potential for improvements to the accounting system and consider their impact on the operation of the organisation.
B   Identify potential areas of fraud arising from control avoidance within the accounting system and grade the risk.
C   Review methods of operating regularly in respect of their cost – effectiveness, reliability and speed.
D   Make recommendations to the appropriate person in a clear, easily understood format.
E   Ensure recommendations to the appropriate person are supported by a clear rationale which includes an explanation of any assumptions made.
F   Explain to those affected the implications of recommended changes in terms of financial costs and benefits.
Range statement:
1.   Weaknesses: Potential for errors Exposure to possible fraud
2.   Accounting system: Manual Computerised
3.   Recommendations: Oral
4.   Changes affecting systems: External regulations Organisational policies and procedures

student notes

17

Knowledge and understanding

The business environment

1 The range of external regulations affecting accounting practice
2 Common types of fraud
3 The implications of fraud

Management techniques

4 Methods for scheduling and planning work
5 Techniques for managing your own time effectively
6 Methods of measuring cost effectiveness
7 Methods of detecting fraud within accounting systems
8 Techniques for influencing and negotiating with decision-makers and controllers of resources
9 Techniques for reviewing recommendations through cost benefit analysis

Management principles and theory

10 Principles of supervision and delegation
11 Principles of fostering effective working relationships, building teams and motivating staff

The organisation

12 How the accounting systems of an organisation are affected by its organisational structure, its Management Information Systems, its administrative systems and procedures and the nature of its business transactions
13 The overview of the organisation's business and its critical external relationships (customers/clients, suppliers, etc)
14 The purpose, structure and the organisation of the accounting function and its relationship with other functions within the organisation
15 Who controls the supply of resources (equipment, materials, information and people) within the organisation

Case Study Advice

If you are completing a report based on the Case Study scenario your assessor will take the place of your work place manager and testify that your work is your own, unaided and authentic.

It is critical therefore that you submit a proposal and drafts to them as your work progresses and get feedback on these.

This aids your assessor in confirming your work is authentic.

If you have a Case Study but have not yet completed the report and want it to be assessed by a different assessor, contact them first. Do not complete the report and then submit it.

There is a possibility that the assessor will ask you to start again as they can not be sure of the authenticity of your work.

FAQs

1) **Does my project need to cover all the standards?** – Yes, your assessor will assess to all the standards of this unit and you will have to map your work to show where each of the standards are covered by page and paragraph number. This will help you ensure your work does cover all the standards.

2) **I completed a project 3 years ago but it was never assessed, can I now submit it for assessment?** – This is a tricky one, and dependent on the circumstances and the assessor. Your assessor will have to be sure that your work is still current (the recommendations still valid, for example) and that the work is authentic – your own, unaided work. They may not be able to assess your work and may ask that you start again based on your current work place or a Case Study.

3) **My manager won't produce an authentication statement, what can I do?** – If you have completed your project on your work place and your manager will not produce an appropriate authenticity statement, signed and dated on company headed paper, you do not have permission to submit your project based on your place of work. Without this statement your assessor must not assess your work and so you would be asked to start your project again, perhaps based on a Case Study. It is vital therefore that you gain your manager's consent before commencing your project using your own work place.

4) **I am completing my project using the Case Study, who is my work place manager and how can they authenticate my work?** – When you complete the project based on the scenario in the Case Study your assessor takes on the role of work place manager and as part of the assessment process they will produce an authenticity statement. It is vital therefore that you submit a proposal and drafts of your work as you complete it so that they are able to testify that the work is your own and unaided.

5) **What is an Assessment Plan and must I complete one?** – An assessment plan is the result of a negotiation between you and your assessor to plan when and how you are going to complete each phase of the project and the submit a final version of your work. It is required under the assessment code of practice and is an invaluable tool to carefully plan in steps how you can complete the overall report. You do not need to keep exactly to the plan, it can be reviewed and updated as you progress.

6) **What is a project proposal and must I complete one?** – A project proposal is where you set out to your assessor, your initial thoughts and ideas regarding your project. It is vital as it ensures that your assessor can judge whether your project will be appropriate and that you are not proposing too large or small an area of the accounting

student notes✒

system to investigate. It allows your assessor to provide you with valuable feedback and support and is a key part of the authentication process.

7) **What is the final interview and what format will it take?** – The final interview is the last part of the assessment process and is where the assessor asks you questions about the work you have produced. It can aid them in authenticating your work and strengthen any minor areas of weakness so that they can be sure of the sufficiency of your competence. It should take the format of an interview, where your assessor will ask you questions and you provide answers. It will be recorded – either written down or voice recorded – and if written you will be asked to confirm that the written evidence is a true reflection of the interview by signing and dating it.

8) **How do I map my work and why must I do so?** – Mapping your work is where you inform the assessor of the page and paragraph number that covers each part of the standards. This is important first, so that you can be sure that all the standards are covered (if you can't map to one of them then you have missed it out and need to add a paragraph to include it!) and also to ensure that you have a good understanding of what you have gained competence in, by producing this work. To map your work take a copy of the standards (see earlier) and reference each page and paragraph number to them.

9) **Can my project be a series of paragraphs, each addressing the standards in turn?** – No. This is not an appropriate way to produce a professional management report and would not be judged as competent as you will have not demonstrated an ability to write one. Instead, your report should be structured around the sections as outlined in this Companion

10) **What is Internal Verification?** – This is an internal quality assurance check. Each AAT Approved Assessment Centre has an internal verifier who is responsible for ensuring that work reported to the AAT as competent has been appropriately assessed and is actually competent. They do this through a variety of processes and you may have your assessed work reviewed or your final interview observed. If they do not agree with an assessment decision this will be communicated to you either by the AAT directly or your assessor and the additional work required to achieve competence will be discussed.

chapter 3:
MANAGEMENT OF PEOPLE

chapter coverage 📖

Element 10.1

✍ Plan work activities to make the optimum use of resources and to ensure that work is completed within agreed timescales.

✍ Review the competence of individuals undertaking work activities and arrange the necessary training.

✍ Communicate work methods and schedules to colleagues in ways that help them to understand what is expected of them.

✍ Monitor work activities sufficiently closely to ensure quality standards are being met.

✍ Encourage colleagues to report to you promptly any problems and queries that are beyond their authority or expertise to resolve, and resolve these where they are within your authority and expertise.

✍ Refer problems and queries to the appropriate person where resolution is beyond your authority or expertise.

KNOWLEDGE AND UNDERSTANDING AND PERFORMANCE CRITERIA COVERAGE

Element 10.1

knowledge and understanding

4   Methods for scheduling and planning work

5   Techniques for managing your own time effectively

10   Principles of supervision and delegation

11   Principles of fostering effective working relationships, building teams and motivating staff

INVESTIGATING MANAGEMENT OF PEOPLE

The management of people section of your report needs to investigate how you and your colleagues are managed within the work place and make recommendations to improve this. This needs to cover the full range of management activities from induction through the communication of work methods and procedures, to appraisals and training and how the quality of your work is reviewed.

The last two performance criteria (G & H) cover a specific requirement for you to investigate how problems and queries are dealt with and whether recommendations can be made to reduce or prevent these from occurring again.

To cover these criteria imagine that you are a management consultant and have been asked to review the systems and procedures in place for managing staff and make recommendations on how these might be improved. This is effectively what the Unit 10 report should do.

Use one particular department or team in this analysis and, if possible, ensure that this links with the system and fraud research detailed later in this Companion.

Investigation 1

Investigate how staff are informed of their duties and responsibilities in the workplace:

- When they start their employment are they given induction training and is it adequate?

If the organisation has a written induction manual for staff include a copy in the appendices of your report. It is part of the evidence of your research.

If it does not then you have your first recommendation – well done!

- Do they have set procedures in place and checklists and deadlines for key periods such as month end?

Investigate how staff manage their own time:

- Do they use diaries, to-do lists etc?
- Does this work effectively?

Investigate how the quality of their work is assessed on a daily, weekly, monthly and annual basis:

- Does the organisation have an appraisal system?

If the organisation has an appraisal system include a copy in the appendices of your report. It is part of the evidence of your research.

If it does not then you have a recommendation – well done!

- How often does this formal review take place and is it adequate?
- Are any activities double-checked by management before approval?

- Are any documents countersigned at month end?
- How else is the quality of work reviewed and assessed?

Investigate how staff training needs are met by management:

- How are training needs identified?
- What follow up takes place to ensure that any potential needs are met by training and that the training, once received, produces the required effect in improving performance and morale?

Investigate how staff are motivated:

- Is there a good team culture within the organisation?
- Are staff motivated, is there good morale?
- What activities take place to build teams / motivate staff?

Can you make recommendations to improve any of the above?

REPORT: CURRENT PRACTICES AND IMPROVEMENTS

To write up the outcomes of this research into your report write one to two pages detailing the current systems in place for the management of staff and your recommendations to improve them, clearly explaining why and how you have come to these conclusions.

Your report must be written in the third person only (that is no 'I' or 'we' or 'he' or 'she' – and you must not mention any member of staff by name, only job title. Each page and paragraph should be individually numbered.

Write it in a series of short paragraphs showing each area of investigation. When you have completed it you should be able to map your work to the standards – see Chapter 8 on mapping your work to help you with this.

Then ensure you include copies of all documents referred to in your report (appraisals, to-do lists and so on) in your appendices. This is important reference material and if you put yourself into the place of your manager reading the final report it is important to be able to refer to these if required.

Checklist

- Write up your research of each area of investigation as outlined above
- Include copies of all relevant documents in the appendices
- Write only in the third person
- Include recommendations to improve the management of people
- Ensure you have short, individually numbered paragraphs
- Map your work to the standards

---

student notes✍

Investigation 2

Keep a query log:

- To finish this section and meet the needs of the last two performance criteria you then need to consider queries that staff come to you with over a period of time – allow at least one week.

- A good idea would be to keep a log of these and ensure that you include information that helps you meet the requirements of the standards – ie how you were able to deal with the queries, either by yourself, or by referring them to another person in the organisation (include who and why).

- If you feel that your role in work does not enable you to complete this in sufficient detail then you could consider asking your manager to let you shadow them and that staff queries are directed to you over a set period of time. You can then keep a log of this information.

REPORT: OUTCOMES: PROBLEMS AND QUERIES

Write a paragraph in your report to briefly explain the queries that you were able to deal with and how you addressed them and a paragraph on the queries you were not able to deal with – including to whom you referred them and why.

Put your query log into the appendices and refer to it as necessary.

From this research you should be able to make some conclusions about the queries you have investigated or referred to others:

Perhaps some training of staff would prevent such queries arising in the future or procedures can be written or amended?

Not all queries can be addressed in this way but often some simple action can be taken to ensure that such issues do not occur again. This can then be for the benefit of both staff and the organisation.

Checklist

- Keep a log of queries
- Include examples you can and can't deal with
- Put the log in the appendices
- Write a summary in the main report
- Refer to the appendices
- Write short, individually numbered paragraphs
- Write only in the third person
- Make recommendations to prevent future problems and queries

Case Study Advice

When you have read the Case Study through you will notice some areas of the required research outlined above are clearly mentioned and some are not. Consider the Case Study to be a story about an organisation, so areas not covered perhaps do not feature in the organisation at present.

For example: if appraisals or induction are not mentioned then perhaps the organisation does not have them and so you already have some recommendations for improvement.

To enable you to cover the standards on queries you could consider that the problems and queries that the organisation experience are bought to you to resolve. Some you will be able to (and it may include in the Case Study how this was done) and some will have to be referred to senior management.

Immerse yourself in the scenario and remember that the report must read in the same way as if it were your actual workplace. Use your skills, knowledge and imagination to supplement the case scenario and to make detailed recommendations clearly explaining the benefit to the organisation.

The sample report at the back of this Companion will aid your understanding as to how to complete this. Remember to send your draft to your assessor for review – it will aid their authentication of your work and provide you with valuable feedback on your progress.

FAQs

1) **My manager is not keen for me to investigate how people are managed for confidentiality reasons, what can I do?** – You need to discuss this first with your manager. It should be made clear that you are only investigating the processes currently in place and making recommendations to improve them. The report should be impersonal and not refer to specific people and therefore should not breach confidentiality. It can also be pointed out that the assessor, Internal Verifier and other quality assurance processes fully respect that once work has been submitted it is confidential and is not published or shared with others. If your manager is still unwilling then discuss this with your assessor as a Case Study may be a more appropriate basis for your report.

2) **I work in a very large accounts team – do I need to investigate all the team?** – No. It would be expected that many of the areas to investigate, such as inductions and appraisals, are standard across the whole team so can be investigated quite easily by focusing on a small selection. For how people manage their time look first at company or team-wide approaches such as month end schedules

and planners and then take a snap shot of how individuals manage their time, such as diaries, to-do lists or nothing at all. You may conclude for example, that all staff should be issued with diaries as these prove effective or that daily / weekly / monthly planners are constructed for all.

3) **I work in a very small team – there are less than four of us – what should I do?** – This all depends on exactly how many of you there are and what standard procedures and practices there are in place. All staff should receive inductions and appraisals no matter the size of the team and controls need to be thought through very carefully when small teams exist to ensure that appropriate proceedures are in place. You can also investigate time management for a small team if the team consists of just one or two staff. If the organisation is very small this should be discussed with your assessor to ensure that it is an appropriate basis for your report. If not, the Case Study may be a better option on which to base your project.

4) **I am not in a supervisory position at work – how can I cover all the standards?** – This does not matter and although it would be expected that you are in a position to research the areas outlined in this Companion and produce a query log this may be by shadowing your own supervisor for a period of time. If you genuinely feel you are not able to evidence your competence, discuss this with your assessor as the Case Study may be more appropriate.

5) **My company is very informally managed and we don't have appraisals, induction etc – how can I produce this report?** – If these basic tools of people management are not currently in place in your organisation then this is good news as you have your first recommendations – to implement them! Remember that to cover this sufficiently you must make sure your recommendations are detailed, and include the topics that should be covered at induction, or how often an appraisal should be carried out and give a recommended approach. All of this can be researched on the Internet. Don't forget to think about the costs and benefits to the organisation of carrying out such activities.

6) **Any recommendations I come up with are never going to be implemented by my organisation, so what should I do?** – This does not matter. The outcome of Unit 10 should be a professional management report making recommendations to improve the organisation. They do not have to be implemented and while it is hoped that they would at least be reviewed and considered by management, this does not actually have to happen.

7) **My organisation has all these people management tools in place – so there would be no recommendations to improve** – This is fine as long as you can demonstrate to your assessor that you have fully researched all of the areas of investigation and from that research you have concluded that there are no improvements to be made.

chapter 4:
ANALYSIS OF AN ACCOUNTING SYSTEM

chapter coverage 📖

Element 10.2

✍ Identify weaknesses and potential for improvements to the accounting system and consider their impact on the operation of the organisation.

✍ Make recommendations to the appropriate person in a clear, easily understood format.

✍ Ensure recommendations are supported by a clear rationale which includes an explanation of any assumptions made.

KNOWLEDGE AND UNDERSTANDING AND PERFORMANCE CRITERIA COVERAGE

Element 10.2

range statement

1. *Weaknesses:*
    Potential for errors
    Exposure to possible fraud

2. *Accounting system:*
    Manual
    Computerised

3. *Recommendations:*
    Oral
    Written

knowledge and understanding

1   The range of external regulations affecting accounting practice

4   Techniques for influencing and negotiating with decision-makers and controllers of resources

INVESTIGATING AN ACCOUNTING SYSTEM

In this section of report you are required to analyse part of the accounting system in your organisation (both computerised and manual processes) and make recommendations to improve this.

This can be your own role at work or the work of your department of team. It could also be one part of your role – especially if you work in a small team where you each take on several processes or functions.

For example, you may wish to investigate the purchase ledger function in your organisation, or credit control or payroll.

Whichever you choose it should be of sufficient value to the organisation (petty cash or expenses would not be sufficient unless they account for a large amount of expenditure in the organisation and take up a significant amount of staff's time).

The system you choose should ideally be linked to the fraud section later in your report. You will have to be careful here to only include recommendations that improve the overall working of the system – keep improved controls for later when you analyse and investigate the potential for fraud. You can investigate each process separately if this is more appropriate based on your organisation and its structure.

If in doubt discuss this with your assessor and include your approach in your project proposal to ensure you receive appropriate feedback and support.

Again, you need to consider yourself to be a consultant in the work place. You should analyse in detail how the process you have chosen operates and what the key outcomes of it are.

Investigation 1

All processes consist of a series of inputs that are processed into outputs. In a payroll process the input will be the staff hours worked, pay scales etc. The process would be to calculate the payroll and then the output would be that the staff are paid.

Each stage of this process should be analysed in detail and to aid you in this it may be appropriate to **draw a system flow chart**. This shows the key decision making processes, inputs and outputs simply and can be included in the appendices of your report.

System flow chart:

There are many methods to drawing a flow chart with symbols to show each stage of the process and what is a decision or a manual input etc. Although these methods are appropriate, and can be used if you have studied them in the past, a simple flow chart can also be used that clearly shows the flow of the system using boxes and text.

For example:

The system flow chart in Chapter 2 explained the assessment process of your project report. It shows each stage in the process and the key activity that takes place.

REPORT: SYSTEMS FLOW CHART

In the analysis of an accounting system section of your report write a summary of the processes that take place within your chosen system.

Make reference to the flow chart in your appendices.

Checklist

- Decide on the system or part of the system you wish to investigate
- Draw a system flow chart for the appendices
- Write a summary in the main report
- Refer to the appendices
- Write short, individually numbered paragraphs
- Write only in the third person

Investigation 2

SWOT analysis

Another tool to aid you to analyse the system in detail is a SWOT analysis. SWOT stands for:

Strengths
Weaknesses
Opportunities
Threats

The **Strengths** and **Weaknesses** to a system will be internal factors that either make it particularly effective or demonstrate clear weaknesses within it.

An example strength may be that a payroll system is operated by knowledgeable and experienced staff and a weakness might be that is a manual process, dependent on manual calculation which presents many opportunities for human error.

Once strengths and weaknesses have been identified then recommendations can be considered to address the weaknesses.

Opportunities and **Threats** are external to the actual system itself. It may be an opportunity to train more staff in payroll qualifications and a threat that information and legislation relating to payroll is subject to frequent change (tax codes, tax rates, NI contributions etc).

It is sometimes harder to identify external factors such as these but you should try and consider as many as you can – they will also suggest recommendations to improve the system.

Activity

Consider your own organisation or study centre – what are its overall strengths and weaknesses? What are the external opportunities and threats? Detail as many as you can in the SWOT format below:

Strengths	Weaknesses
Opportunities	**Threats**

REPORT: SWOT ANALYSIS

In the analysis of an accounting system section of your report write a summary of the SWOT analysis focusing on the weaknesses identified in the system. Make reference to the SWOT in the appendices.

Checklist

- Complete a SWOT analysis on your chosen system or part of a system
- Put the SWOT in the appendices
- Write a summary in the main report
- Refer to the appendices
- Write short, individually numbered paragraphs
- Write only in the third person

Investigation 3

PEST analysis

A final tool that may assist you is a PEST analysis. A PEST analysis investigates 4 factors that may affect your organisation and the system you have chosen to analyse. These 4 factors are:

Political

Economic

Social

Technological

Political factors – There are a variety of political factors that can affect the operation of an accounting system. These might include the following:

- Changes in NIC rates
- Changes in VAT rates
- Changes in company legislation regarding publication of financial statements
- Changes in financial reporting standards

Economic factors – Examples of economic factors that might affect the accounting system are:

- Increase/decrease in the volume of transactions due to general or specific changes in the economy and customer demands
- Changes in the availability and wage rate of the labour force
- The staff available to work in the accounting function
- The budget applied to the accounting function

If the general or specific economic changes for an organisation lead to an increase or decrease in the general level of transactions then this will have a direct effect on the number of transactions within an accounting function although not necessarily on the nature of those transactions or the method of operations.

Social factors – Social factors that might affect the accounting system might include the following:

- Changing work patterns such as flexitime and home working
- Family commitments leading to changes such as part time working and job sharing
- Employment legislation

Technological factors – Examples of technological factors that might cause changes in the accounts system might be:

- Advances in computer technology
- Security issues
- Technological fraud
- On-line banking

REPORT: PEST ANALYSIS

In the analysis of an accounting system section of your report write a summary of the PEST analysis and make reference to it in the appendices. You now should have completed enough research into the chosen accounting system to be able to make some recommendations for improvement.

Write detailed recommendations at the end of this section.

Checklist

- Complete a PEST analysis on your chosen system or part of a system
- Put the PEST in the appendices
- Write a summary in the main report
- Refer to the appendices
- Write recommendations resulting from your investigation into the system
- Write short, individually numbered paragraphs
- Write only in the third person

Remember that your recommendations do not have to be implemented – the purpose of your report is to investigate and analyse the key areas and to make recommendations to improve them – not to have these recommendations put into place.

The **Performance Criteria** for this unit ask that you make your recommendations clear, in an easily understood format and that they are supported by a clear rationale as to why you have concluded that they are appropriate. In order to demonstrate competence in this you are required to fully justify *all* your recommendations, not just those relating to this section, plus summarise them in the executive summary (explained later in Chapter 7).

The **range statements** for these Performance Criteria ensure you cover a range of weaknesses that you identify. This range is to:

- Identify weaknesses that lead to the potential for errors;
- And those that might result in the possibility of fraud.

The potential for fraud is covered later in a chapter on its own (see Chapter 5) so for now you should ensure that your completed work does include at least *one* weakness that could result in errors (perhaps a highly manual process) and a recommendation to improve it. When mapping your work (see Chapter 8) you should clearly map this range statement to the appropriate weakness and recommendation.

The range statements also ask that your recommendations be presented to management:

- In a written format (your report);
- and orally.

There are two ways that you can demonstrate that you have presented them orally to either management or your assessor.

If you are writing your project based on the work place then your manager's authenticity statement can include that your recommendations have been discussed orally with them and you can map the range statement to this.

The alternative (and your assessor may include this anyway) is for you to discuss and explain them with your assessor as part of the final interview which your assessor must undertake as the final part of the assessment process.

The final **range statement** covered by this section of your report is regarding a manual and computerised system. Your research through your system flow chart and your system SWOT must make reference to both manual and computerised parts of your chosen system.

The two **Knowledge and Understanding statements** covered by this chapter are to:

- Demonstrate a knowledge of the range of external regulations affecting the accounting function

- Demonstrate knowledge and understanding of the techniques required to influence and negotiate with decision makers.

Both your report, with its executive summary, and your ability to discuss orally your recommendations will demonstrate this knowledge. Part of a PEST analysis is to investigate regulations that affect the system you are analysing.

Ensure you clearly include this in your report and you can then map the relevant knowledge and understanding statement to the relevant paragraph.

Case Study Advice

The Case Study contains a lot of information about the whole accounting function in the organisation and you are not expected to write this section of your report on all of it.

Instead, read it through carefully and decide on one section of the system (perhaps Payroll or Purchase Ledger) to analyse, ideally ensuring you will also investigate this part of the system in your fraud section. Perhaps pick the one of which you have the most practical experience or the one that appears to have the most room for improvement.

If in doubt discuss this with your assessor and remember that if the detail contained within the case scenario is weak then you can supplement it with your own research or knowledge of the work place. Also remember to ensure that the report reads as if you work in the organisation and are making the recommendations to your own manager.

The requirement to discuss the recommendations orally will be covered by your assessor as part of the final interview to aid them both to ensure your competence and to authenticate your work.

FAQs

1) **I am not sure what part of the accounting system to investigate – which should I choose?** – This depends on your particular organisation and accounting system. The system you choose to investigate should not be so large that it will take you months of research and take pages to document and not so small that it is not sufficient in importance in your organisation. A good guide would be to consider the size of your organisation and the number of staff working on the various systems and processes. Anything that takes up a small amount of one member of staff's time is probably too small. Any system that takes several staff to operate could be too large. If in doubt discuss this with your assessor.

2) **I want to investigate more than one system – is this OK?** – This is dependent on the size of the system(s) and the amount of work involved. Remember that the overall finished report should be approximately between 3,500-4,500 words (excluding the appendices) and that you do not want to spend to long on this section of your report as you have 3 other key sections to complete. If your organisation has requested that you investigate several areas and this is going to add practical value to your finished report then discuss this with your assessor.

3) **I am investigating the system in this section so then how do I keep this separate from fraud?** – This is a tricky area as you ideally want to keep the same area of investigation for both the analysis of

the accounting system and the fraud sections. A key point to remember is that in this section your focus is on the procedures and processes that make up how the system actually operates and how these can be improved to make the system more efficient and effective. The fraud section will focus on the controls in place and whether they are adequate.

4) **How should I draw my system flow chart?** – The key answer to this is simply. A detailed flow chart is not required. Your aim is to map the processes and flow of the system so that the reader of your report can gain an understanding of how the system works.

5) **Why should I put the flow chart, SWOT and PEST analysis in the appendices and not in the main report** – A professional report such as this should not include any tables, charts or diagrams. These are kept to the appendices to be referred to when required. It also helps keep your word count down!

6) **I am struggling to think of opportunities and threats to my system, what can I do?** – You could address this section by asking your supervisor or manager to suggest some. Another idea is to conduct a little research into the overall environment in which the organisation operates. If after these two possibiities you are still finding this difficult then do not worry as including the strengths and weaknesses are far more important.

7) **Any recommendations I come up with are never going to be implemented by my organisation so what should I do?** – This does not matter. The outcome of Unit 10 should be a professional management report making recommendations to improve the organisation. They do not have to be implemented and while it is hoped that they would at least be reviewed and considered by management this does not actually have to happen.

8) **My organisation has really efficient and effective systems in place – so there would be no recommendations to improve** – This is fine as long as you can demonstrate to your assessor that you have fully researched all of the areas of investigation and from that research you have concluded that there are no improvements to be made.

chapter 5:
FRAUD CONTROLS

chapter coverage 📖

Element 10.2

✍ Identify potential areas of fraud arising from control avoidance within the accounting system and grade the risk.

KNOWLEDGE AND UNDERSTANDING AND PERFORMANCE CRITERIA COVERAGE

Element 10.2

knowledge and understanding

2   Common types of fraud

3   The implications of fraud

7   Methods of detecting fraud in an accounting system

INVESTIGATION OF FRAUD CONTROLS

This section can be covered by further investigation of the accounting system you have already analysed for the accounting system section of your report or by analysing a different part of the accounting function.

To gain competence you are required to investigate all the potential for fraudulent activity within that part of the system, the controls already in place to prevent fraud from taking place, and to conclude as to whether the controls are adequate, or can be improved in some way.

WHAT IS FRAUD?

Fraud is deception of some sort which in a company situation will involve either:

- Misappropriation of assets
- Misstatement of the financial statements

Misappropriation of assets

This in its simplest form is the theft of assets such as cash or stock. However there are a variety of different and subtle ways in which this can be accomplished:

- Theft of cash
- Theft of stock
- Teeming and lading
- Fictitious employees
- Fictitious suppliers
- Fictitious customers
- Collusion with customers
- Collusion with suppliers
- Receipt of invoices for bogus supply of goods or services
- Disposal of assets
- Pension funds

Misstatement of the financial statements

In this type of fraud the financial statements are deliberately manipulated in order to falsify the position of the company. This could be by over-stating assets or profits or by under-stating the results and the profits.

Examples of this type of fraud are:

- Over-valuation of stock
- Window dressing

- Not writing off bad debts
- Manipulation of depreciation charges
- Fictitious sales
- Understating expenses

These lists are not exhaustive, you should try to think of any possibilities of fraud within your chosen system.

Investigation 1

Consider all the probable frauds that could occur within your chosen system – even if the controls currently in place do not make it very likely or possible.

By doing this you will demonstrate your knowledge and understanding as to the common types of fraud that could occur.

Then investigate the controls currently in place to prevent each from occurring.

Then conclude as to the risk to the organisation that it might be defrauded in that way.

Grade that risk to the organisation, perhaps 1 = low and 5=high

A simple way to analyse this would be to construct a fraud matrix – which could then be included in your appendices.

A simple matrix could look like the following:

Potential fraud	Controls currently in place	Risk to organisation	Implications	Improvement identified
1.				
2.				
3.				

To ensure you cover this section to the required sufficiency you should ensure that you include at least 5 potential frauds in your research.

REPORT: FRAUD MATRIX

In the Fraud Controls section of your report write a summary of the findings from the completion of the Fraud Matrix and make reference to it in the appendices

As part of your write-up of this section be sure to include general and specific controls in place. General controls include supervision and internal audit whereas specific controls might be counter-signatures or the need for receipts.

Then make recommendations to improve the current controls if this is appropriate.

Checklist

- Complete a Fraud Matrix on your chosen system or part of a system
- Grade the risk to the organisation of each fraud occurring
- Put the Matrix in the appendices
- Write a summary in the main report
- Refer to the appendices
- Make recommendations to improve the current controls, where appropriate
- Write short, individually numbered paragraphs
- Write only in the third person

Case Study Advice

As with the accounting system section you should pick one area of the Case Study scenario to cover for this section.

If the specific information contained within the scenario is weak then supplement it with your own research or knowledge of the work place (for example, you may need to research good controls that should be in place within a purchase ledger system) and discuss this with your assessor if unsure.

FAQs

1) **My company has good controls and fraud is unlikely, how can I complete this section?** – Within this section you are investigating all the possible frauds that could occur and analysing the current controls to determine whether they are adequate or not. From this you can conclude as to whether there are recommendations to make to improve the controls. If you conclude that there are no recommendations as good controls exist then this is acceptable.

2) **Can the fraud risk matrix go in the body of the report?** – You should keep all tables, charts and diagrams in the appendices to a professional report and make reference to them in the body of the report.

3) **How can I grade the risk of the fraud occurring?** – To do this contrast your own, simple, grading system. Perhaps a grade of 1 = low risk of occurring and 5 = high risk of occurring.

4) **How can I research possible frauds in my chosen system?** – One way of doing this is to work backwards, start at the controls in place and then investigate what they could possibly be in place to prevent.

You could also research the Internet using a search engine and searching for examples of your chosen system fraud. i.e. you could search for 'examples of purchase ledger fraud'.

5) **Any recommendations I come up with are never going to be implemented by my organisation so what should I do?** – This does not matter. The outcome of Unit 10 should be a professional management report making recommendations to improve the organisation. They do not have to be implemented and while it is hoped that they would at least be reviewed and considered by management this does not actually have to happen.

chapter 6:
CONTINGENCY PLANNING

chapter coverage 📖

Element 10.1

✎ Prepare, in collaboration with management, contingency plans to meet possible emergencies.

✎ Co-ordinate work activities effectively and in accordance with work plans and contingency plans.

KNOWLEDGE AND UNDERSTANDING AND PERFORMANCE CRITERIA COVERAGE

Element 10.1

range statement

1   Contingency plans allowing for:

Fully functioning computer system not being available
Staff absence
Changes in work patterns and demands

CONTINGENCY PLANNING

Contingency planning will involve assessing unplanned events which may occur from time to time. The assessment will involve determining the following:

- The probability of the event happening
- The level of impact of the event happening

If there is a reasonable probability of the event happening and the effect on the business would be material then a contingency plan should normally be considered.

Note that the Performance Criteria for this section has a range statement attached to it and you are required to ensure that you research, and report on, your organisation's current contingency plans for:

- Staff absence
- Loss of IT systems
- Changes in work patterns and demands

Investigation 1

In order to sufficiently cover these standards you need to investigate fully the current plans in place for the 3 range statements and to conclude as to whether they are adequate and appropriate.

If not you then need to make detailed recommendations as to how they can be improved.

It is not sufficient to make general statements as to how the organisation will cover an event such as loss of staff or IT systems and a good way to ensure that you have tested fully the sufficiency of such a plan is to test it in practice – either hypothetically or in reality.

There is little point in an organisation having a plan in place if it is not tested to see if it works. Without such a test you may find that at the critical moment the plan does not work, perhaps for some simple reason that has been overlooked.

Staff absence

What if a key member of staff was absent from work due to an illness or accident. If it were to be for only a few days it may be that your organisation would cover this absence with other staff. You should however, consider fully the practicalities of this. For, example consider the following:

- What if the other staff are unable or unwilling to work extra hours to cover the work?
- What work would be deemed critical and must be completed to a deadline and what could be left until the absent employee returns to work?
- Are staff trained to cover this work?

- Would other staff completing this work mean a reduction in the controls in place?
- How would the extra work be shared among the staff?

All these practicalities need to be included as part of the plan and then should be extended to cover long-term absence as it is then much harder to cover with existing staff, especially if this means working additional hours for an extended period of time.

In your investigation you need to ensure you cover both long- and short-term absence of staff and loss of IT systems and this is the area of your report that you may need to ask your manager for assistance in order to complete it fully if your organisation's plans are your starting point for your research.

If none exist then you clearly already have some good recommendations for improvement.

Loss of IT systems

The loss of IT systems also needs to include hardware and software loss as they both have different implications to the organisation.

Just as you have to investigate the current plans in place in sufficient detail you must also ensure your recommendations are thought through. For example, you may suggest a back-up of your system is taken each evening to prevent your organisation suffering if your current computer system is lost. Factors to consider with this would be:

- Who is responsible for the back-up and who would cover this if they were absent?
- What checks should be in place to ensure it takes place?
- Where would the back-up be stored?
- If the hardware is also lost to where would the back-up be restored?
- Has it been checked that the back-up can be physically restored to the system?

Your recommendations should be in sufficient detail as to demonstrate your knowledge and understanding of this area.

Changes in work patterns and demands

For this third range statement you then need to consider your organisation's current contingency plans to cope with either a significant increase or decrease in work demand of the accounting system and/or a change to working patterns – perhaps brought about by changes in working legislation.

Does your organisation have plans in place to identify and implement new working regulations such as paternity leave?

If not, then it could be exposed to issues regarding staff absence and tribunal claims.

How does the organisation identify that staff workload has increased or decreased significantly and plan to either increase or decrease staff numbers?

For example, a new marketing campaign may result in a significant increase in orders and therefore the work of the sales ledger team.

How does the organisation plan for this? If plans are not currently in place then this is where you need to ensure you have recommendations to improve this.

Co-ordination of work plans

To complete this section and cover Performance Criteria 10.1F conduct an investigation into what happened in your organisation when one of the contingency plans had to be put into place. Perhaps a member of staff was absent or the computer system failed. Investigate whether all went to plan and whether any improvements to the plans can be made.

REPORT: CONTINGENCY PLANNING: LOSS OF STAFF AND IT

Write up the findings of your investigation to clearly include the current plans in place across the range statements.

Ensure staff absence and the loss of IT is covered for both the short and long terms.

Then make recommendations to improve the current plans if this is appropriate.

Checklist

- Complete an investigation into the current plans in place
- Cover the full range statements
- Investigate both short- and long-term planning
- Make recommendations to improve the current plans, where appropriate
- Write short, individually numbered paragraphs
- Write only in the third person

Case Study Advice

Depending on the Case Study you receive you may have a lot or a little information about the contingency planning currently taking place in the organisation.

You will be required to cover all three of the range statements in the same way that a report based on a work place will. To do this you may need to research contingency planning and bring in your own knowledge and experience – with some common sense!

To consider staff absence ensure you think about all the plans in place, or recommendations, fully. Think about how temporary or new staff could pick up work practices quickly and how work could be allocated.

To consider IT you need to research the types of contingency plans available to organisations. These might include off site back up, duplicate servers or insurance schemes that provide duplicate offices in case of complete loss of premises.

For changes in work patterns and demands consider how you would plan to recognise and take action on a significant change in the workload of the department. Think all your ideas through to ensure your recommendations are robust and sufficient.

FAQs

1) **I do not know what contingency plans are in place in my organisation – how can I research this?** – This depends on your particular organisation. The best places to start would be your supervisor or manager and the IT support you receive. They should be able to inform you of what plans are currently in place.

2) **My organisation has no formal plans – staff absence is dealt with informally when it occurs** – Great! – You have a recommendation to improve! Plans help an organisation stay in control when an event such as a key member of staff is absent, especially at a critical time such as month end. If a plan is in place then all staff know what their part is in ensuring the work is completed and what work is necessary and what can be left until the member of staff returns.

3) **Our IT is outsourced to a third party organisation, how can I research this?** – Your organisation should be aware of the plans in place to ensure that your systems are maintained and when they fail that they are up and running again as soon as possible. Your department will also have plans in place to ensure that while the IT system is down business continues to operate. If there are none then this should be considered as a recommendation.

4) **How do I cover changes in work patterns and demands?** – This range statement looks at how your organisation plans to cope with changes, perhaps to legislation such as paternity leave, and plans to cope with significant increases or decreases to demand. Discuss this with your supervisor. It may be that the HR department are responsible for implementing changes in employment law and your Financial Controller responsible for changes in accounting regulations. It may also be that when excessive overtime is worked on a regular basis a decision is made, and approved, to appoint additional staff. If still in doubt about this area then discuss this with your assessor.

5) **Any recommendations I come up with are never going to be implemented by my organisation so what should I do?** – This does not matter. The outcome of Unit 10 should be a professional management report making recommendations to improve the organisation. They do not have to be implemented and while it is hoped that they would at least be reviewed and considered by management this does not actually have to happen.

6) **My organisation has really efficient and effective plans in place – so there would be no recommendations to improve** – This is fine as long as you can demonstrate to your assessor that you have fully researched all of the areas of investigation and from that research you have concluded that there are no improvements to be made.

chapter 7:
PULLING IT ALL TOGETHER

—————— chapter coverage 📖 ——————

Element 10.2

✍ Review methods of operating regularly in response of their cost-effectiveness, reliability and speed.

✍ Explain to those affected the implications of recommended changes in terms of financial costs and benefits.

KNOWLEDGE AND UNDERSTANDING AND PERFORMANCE CRITERIA COVERAGE

Element 10.2

range statement

Changes affecting the system:

Organisational policies and procedures

knowledge and understanding

6   Methods of measuring cost effectiveness

9   Techniques for reviewing recommendations through cost benefit analysis

12   How the accounting systems of an organisation are affected by its organisational structure, its Management Information Systems, its administrative systems and procedures and the nature of its business transactions

13   The overview of the organisation's business and its critical external relationships (customers/clients, suppliers, etc)

14   The purpose, structure and the organisation of the accounting function and its relationship with other functions within the organisation

15   Who controls the supply of resources (equipment, materials, information and people) within the organisation

PULLING IT ALL TOGETHER

This chapter covers the other sections of your report required to pull it together into a completed final report ready for assessment by your assessor. To remind you how it all comes together the sections of the full report are:

- Title Page
- Contents Page
- Executive Summary
- Introduction to the Organisation
- Terms of Reference
- Methodology
- Management of People
- Analysis of an Accounting system
- Fraud Controls
- Contingency Planning
- Cost Benefit Analysis
- Appendices

You now have completed the 4 main areas of your report and made some recommendations to improve the organisation's management of people, controls to prevent fraud, part of the accounting system and contingency planning.

We will now look at each of the remaining sections in turn. Apart from the first two, the Title page and the Contents page, each must be included as numbered sections to your report with the individual paragraphs numbered as per the guidance in the rest of this chapter.

Title page

The title page of your report should contain a meaningful title, your full name and your AAT student registration number. It is also recommended that it includes a statement of authenticity, that the report is your own, unaided work, and that this is signed and dated by yourself.

A meaningful title might be:

> *An investigation into the Management of People, Purchase Ledger System, Fraud Controls and Contingency Planning at XYZ plc.*

Yours should reflect both the name of your organisation and the system you have chosen to investigate.

Contents page

This should set out the page and section number of each part of your report. It is also recommended that you include a word count on this page of the total number of words in your report, excluding the appendices.

Most word processing packages include a word count facility. To check the word count in Microsoft Word click on Tools, Word Count and the total number of words will be calculated.

An example contents page would look like this:

Contents

Section:		Page:
1.	Executive Summary	2
2.	Introduction to the organisation	3
3.	Terms of Reference	4
4.	Methodology	5
5.	Management of People	6
6.	Analysis of an Accounting System	8
7.	Fraud Controls	10
8.	Contingency Planning	12
9.	Cost Benefit Analysis	13
10.	Appendices	15

Word Count: 4256 words

Executive summary

This is a short, summarised version of the overall report that sets out the main findings for the reader.

> Imagine that you have commissioned a report into a possible re-structuring of your company and have recruited some consultants to do this for you – they have produced for you a 10,000 word report detailing their findings, recommendations and rationale behind them.
>
> Although you would probably want to read through the full report at some stage you would also want a summarised version to set the overall scene before you do so, detailing the main recommendations and a brief explanation of why they have been identified.

This is what an executive summary does. For your report it should be no more than one page long and should summarise your main recommendations and reasons for them.

This does repeat the recommendations which you will also include in your main report but this is important to set the scene for your reader before they become involved with the detail. They should be covered very briefly in the Summary section.

Your executive summary also must refer to your **Cost Benefit Analysis** (see below) as this is an important part of summarising the overall costs and benefits of the recommendations made.

To meet one of the specific Performance Criteria, you should also include at the end of your executive summary a conclusion as to how often you recommend an investigation and report such as this to be carried out by the organisation and why.

Introduction to the organisation

This section explains to the reader of the report the background to the organisation and its accounts team and system(s) to put the overall report into context.

As this section covers some specific knowledge and understanding ensure you include the following briefly:

- The organisation's background, history, size and owners

- The organisation's overall structure (include an organisation chart in the appendices)

- The nature of the organisation's business – what does it do?

- Examples of key customers and suppliers to the organisation

- Where the accounts team are based and its structure (include an organisation and an accounts division chart in the appendices)

- How the accounts team interacts and communicates with the rest of the organisation – are they integrated with the rest of the organisation or in a separate office?

This section should be no more than one page in length so as above, each point must only be covered briefly, perhaps in a sentence or two.

Terms of reference

This should be a short section that explains to the reader exactly what the report sets out to do. It explains why it is being written and what areas it covers.

The terms of reference the Unit 10 report can also include that you are completing the report as part of your Technician level studies. This would not be included in a professional business report but is relevant to why you have produced this work and can be included here.

As with the whole report none of this should be written in the first person so there should be no 'I' or 'my' in this. An example of suitable text is included in the sample report at the back of this Companion.

Methodology

This sets out the research carried out into the project and how it was completed.

As with the rest of the work it should be entirely in the third person.

For example

Instead of:

'In order to determine the Management of People I carried out a questionnaire with each of the team'

State:

'In order to determine the Management of People a questionnaire was completed by each member of the accounts team'

Or instead of:

'I reviewed past internal audit reports'

State:

'Past internal audit reports were viewed'

Cost Benefit Analysis

The Cost Benefit Analysis (CBA) takes your recommendations and analyses them in terms of the costs and benefits to the organisation of implementing them.

Both costs and benefits can be explained in terms of tangible and intangible terms:

Tangible – these are costs and benefits that are easy to value, either in terms of time and/or money.

For example, if recommending a new computer system then tangible costs would include:

- The cost of the system itself
- The loss of staff time while they are training
- Other tangible costs to such a system such as future licences and improved speed of processing

---

Wherever possible in your CBA you should include tangible costs with an estimate of them.

You would not be expected to get detailed quotations or information to support your recommendations but you should make estimates as to what the costs will be as this will aid the reader of your report in making any decisions as to whether to implement the recommendations.

> **Intangible** – these are costs and benefits that are much harder to quantify.
>
> For example a new computer system may:
>
> - Improve the motivation and morale of staff.
>
> Although happier, more motivated staff may be more efficient increasing organisational productivity this may be difficult to value in monetary terms.

For all recommendations you have made there should be some intangible costs and/or benefits identified.

These do not have to have estimated values assigned to them but as they are often powerful persuaders for implementing a recommendation they should be included so that the decision maker can consider all the issues fully.

The Cost Benefit Analysis can either go in your report as a new chapter, following on from Fraud Controls and before the Appendices or as an Appendix in itself.

Which approach you choose you do may be influenced by the overall word count of the report so far, remember that this does *not* include the appendices.

Whichever you choose ensure your Cost Benefit Analysis is referred to in your executive summary as it is an important part of the overall report.

chapter 8:
MAPPING TO THE STANDARDS

student notes✍

MAPPING YOUR REPORT TO THE STANDARDS

As part of the assessment process for this unit you are required to map your project and report to the standards.

This should be in the form of page and paragraph number and the reason for this is two-fold:

- You then have a greater understanding of exactly what you are achieving competence in

- You can ensure your work covers all the standards before your final submission

A full set of the standards with a sample mapping approach is included in the sample report at the back of this Companion.

When mapping your work you should list all the paragraphs where that particular Performance Criteria, range or knowledge and understanding is covered.

This Companion lists the relevant standards to each section of the report in the individual chapters to aid you with what each section should cover.

Some of this will be obvious, for example you will have one to two paragraphs that discuss contingency planning for absence so you can easily map these to the relevant Performance Criteria and range statements.

Ensure that if your recommendations also cover a particular part of the standards (for example, you may have made recommendations to improve the contingency plans for absence) you map these in as well.

A good document to use for the mapping is the section of the NVQ student record included on the AAT website at

http://www.aat.org.uk/students/content/item5809/

The standards for Unit 10 can be printed and the relevant page and paragraph numbers can be included next to where each of the standards are covered.

You may find it harder to map some of the knowledge and understanding to your report. Where they are less explicit they may be implied by what you have written.

This is acceptable for some but if you are finding that it is very difficult to map a certain K&U statement it may be because it is not included in your report and it therefore needs further work.

If this is the case then look back through this Companion to where we have referenced that statement and look again at our advice and guidance.

Your assessor will also be a good source of advice and remember that throughout your report you should submit drafts of your work for feedback and support to enable your assessor to be sure that the work is your own and unaided.

Please remember that your project should not be written as a set of answers to each of the Performance Criteria, range and knowledge and understanding.

It is tempting to consider this when looking at the standards and developing your approach to mapping and to ensure your report covers all necessary criteria but the AAT's chief assessor has issued guidance to assessors that any reports structured as a series of paragraphs addressing each of the standards in turn must be rejected as they do not address the formatting needs required by a professional business report.

Once you have mapped your work and all the standards are covered then your report should be ready for final submission to your assessor.

student notes✍

SAMPLE CASE STUDY AND REPORT

APPROACH TO PRODUCING THIS REPORT

As this example report is based around a Case Study it is essential to read the whole case through before deciding how to complete the report. Information required for different sections will be included throughout. A proposal for the report should then be produced and discussed with an assessor to ensure that the overall approach is correct and that a suitable part of the accounting system has been selected for review.

Once this proposal has been submitted and reviewed and discussed with the assessor then each section should be written using the exact same rules and format as required by a student completing the report of their own work place. Each section, once completed, should then be submitted to the assessor for review and feedback.

AUTHENTICITY STATEMENT

This is a Witness testimony that states that the work completed, to the writer's best knowledge, is your own, unaided and that the recommendations contained within it have been discussed orally.

It should be completed on headed paper, be signed and dated by your manager/assessor (see below) and have their full contact details.

If you have completed the project on your work place then this statement **must** be completed by your manager and be on your organisation's headed paper. This effectively not only confirms that the work is your own and unaided, but also gives you permission to use your organisation as the basis of the project.

If you have completed the project on an AAT Case Study then this must be completed by your assessor, on your training organisation's headed paper. In order that they be able to testify the work is your own, and unaided, it is essential that you communicate with them throughout the assessment process with project proposals and drafts.

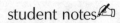

Mapping Sheet

You must complete this fully, showing where each performance criteria, range and knowledge and understanding is included within your project by paragraph number, before we can assess your work.

Name: A student

AAT Registration number: 12345698

Element 10.1	Page*	Paragraph number
A. Plan work activities to make the optimum use of resources and to ensure that work is completed within agreed timescales.		4.1.1 / 4.1.2 / 4.1.3 / 5.12 / 5.17.1 / 5.17.2 / 5.17.3 / 5.17.4
B. Review the competence of individuals undertaking work activities and arrange the necessary training.		4.1.1 / 4.1.2 / 4.1.4 / 4.1.6 / 5.2 – 5.9 / 5.13 / 5.17.5 / 5.17.6
C. Prepare, in collaboration with management, **contingency plans** to meet possible emergencies.		See range
D. Communicate work methods and schedules to colleagues in ways that help them to understand what is expected of them.		4.1.5 / 5.10 / 5.11 / 5.17.7 / 5.17.8 / 5.17.9
E. Monitor work activities sufficiently closely to ensure quality standards are being met.		5.13 / 5.17.5 / 5.16.5
F. Co-ordinate work activities effectively and in accordance with work plans and contingency plans.		4.1.3 / 4.4.1 / 5.14 / 8.5.1
G. Encourage colleagues to report to you promptly any problems and queries that are beyond their authority or expertise to resolve, and resolve these where they are within your authority and expertise.		5.15, Appendix 3
H. Refer problems and queries to the appropriate person where resolution is beyond your authority or expertise.		5.15, Appendix 3
Range Statement		
Contingency plans allowing for: Fully functioning computer system not being available		4.4.3 / 8.2 / 8.5.1 / 8.5.4-6
Staff absence		4.4.1 / 4.4.2 / 8.1 / 8.5.2-3
Changes in work patterns and demands		4.4.1 / 8.3

** Page numbers not included in this example case study – when mapping your work you must include them

Element 10.2	Page *	Paragraph number
A. Identify **Weaknesses** and potential for improvements to the accounting system and consider their impact on the operation of the organisation.		6.1-6.6 / 6.7
B. Identify potential areas of fraud arising from control avoidance within the **accounting system** and grade the risk.		4.3 / 7.1
C. Review methods of operating regularly in respect of their cost – effectiveness, reliability and speed.		4.1.6 / 4.5 / 4.6 / 4.7 / 5.17.10
D. Make **recommendations** to the appropriate person in a clear, easily understood format		4.2.1 / 6.8 / 7.3
E. Ensure **recommendations** to the appropriate person are supported by a clear rationale which includes and explanation of any assumptions made.		4.2.1 / 6.8 / 7.3
F. Explain to those affected the implications of **recommended changes** in terms of financial costs and benefits.		Appendix 6
Range Statement		
1 **Weaknesses:** Potential for errors		6.7.1 / 6.7.1
Exposure to possible fraud		6.7.3 / 7.2.1 / 7.2.2
2 **Accounting system:** Manual		6.7.1
Computerised		6.8.1
3 **Recommendations:** Oral		Managers authenticity Oral Q
Written		Exec Summary 6.8
4 **Changes affecting systems:** External regulations		4.4.4 / 8.5.7
Organisational policies and procedures		7.3.1 / 7.3.2 / 7.3.5 / 7.3.6

** Page numbers not included in this example case study – when mapping your work you must include them

student notes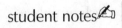

Knowledge and Understanding

You must have demonstrated you both know and understand:

K&U	Reference (page & paragraph)
The Business environment:	
1. The range of external regulations affecting accounting practice	8.3.4
2. Common types of fraud	7.2
3. The implications of fraud	7.1
Management Techniques:	
4. Methods for scheduling and planning work	5.17.1
5. Techniques for managing your own time effectively	5.17.1
6. Methods of measuring cost effectiveness	5.17.10
7. Methods of detecting fraud within accounting systems	7.1
8. Techniques for influencing and negotiating with decision-makers and controllers of resources	Exec Summary
9. Techniques for reviewing recommendations through cost-benefit analysis	Appendix 6
Management Principles and Theory:	
10. Principles of supervision and delegation	5.1 / 5.2-5.3
11. Principles of fostering effective working relationships, building teams and motivating staff	5.17.5 / 5.17.6
The organisation:	
12. How the accounting systems of an organisation are affected by its organisational structure, its Management Information Systems, its administrative systems and procedures and the nature of its business transactions	1.3.1 – 1.3.4 1.4
13. The overview of the organisation's business and its critical external relationships (customers/clients, suppliers, etc)	1.1 / 1.2
14. The purpose, structure and the organisation of the accounting function and its relationship with other functions within the organisation	1.4 / 5.1
15. Who controls the supply of resources (equipment, materials, information and people)within the organisation	1.1

The Case Study

A report into the Management of People, Fraud Controls, Purchasing Ledger system and Contingency Planning in Delmar Electronics Limited

Student Name: A Student
Student Registration Number: 12345698

I certify that this report is my own, unaided work

Signed: A STUDENT

Date: 20/03/XX

student notes✍

Contents

Word Count: 4528

** Page numbers not included in this example case study – when completing your work you must include them

1 Introduction to the organisation

1.1   Delmar Electronics Limited (DEL) has been established for 6 years and is run by a Board of Directors of 4. The business specialises in a high quality, specialist range of semi-conductor test equipment. The Board of Directors are the owners of the business.

1.2   Over the 6 years the organisation has been in business the turnover has grown rapidly to £20 million and the organisation employees over 200 employees.

1.3   DEL's information systems are up to 6 years old and consist of:

1.3.1   Financial Accounting system with integrated general, purchase and sales ledger operating in MSDOS

1.3.2   A stand-alone full absorption costing system that runs on Property Wise software

1.3.3   A new integrated payroll and personnel database management system running in Windows

1.3.4   A computer aided design / computer aided management system, used for the design and control of the production of the test equipment

1.4   DEL's accounts department is run by the Company Accountant, responsible to the Finance Director. The accounts team are based at DEL's one manufacturing site and situated within a central office. They liaise with manufacturing and logistics staff on a daily basis.

2 Terms of Reference

2.1 This report investigates and makes recommendations to improve the management of people, contingency planning and the purchasing ledger system of DEL.

2.2 Within the purchasing system it analyses the system currently in place and the risks contained within it for fraud.

2.3 It also meets the requirements of the AAT Unit 10 Managing Accounting Systems and People assessment.

3   **Methodology**

3.1   In order that this report be written staff were interviewed regarding their own workloads and training needs. The results of these interviews are included as appendix 4 to this report.

3.2   A review of company HR policies and practices also took place.

3.3   To investigate the purchase ledger system a system flow chart and SWOT analysis were completed and are included in appendices 1 and 2.

3.4   Fraud controls were analysed through a team meeting where staff were requested to consider potential frauds within the purchase ledger system and the current controls in place to prevent them were discussed.

3.5   A log of queries and problems raised with the accounting technician was compiled and reviewed in order to identify recommendations that would prevent such issues arising again.

3.6   Contingency plans in place were reviewed along with critical incidents that had occurred at DEL.

4   Executive Summary

4.1   This report includes a detailed investigation of the **management of people** within DEL and makes the following key recommendations:

4.1.1   Year end schedules and plans should be fully reviewed and staff should be trained in time management.

4.1.2   The work of the general ledger clerk should be reviewed and spread evenly over the month or partnered with another clerk in the office.

4.1.3   DEL should consider moving the financial year end to a period that does not clash with the payroll year end and a policy of not authorising annual leave during busy periods.

4.1.4   A system of staff appraisals should be implemented and a policy created for staff who wish to undertake training.

4.1.5   A procedures manual should be created for each role and an induction programme should be developed. Job descriptions should also be implemented.

4.1.6   DEL should implement a review of systems and processes on a regular basis.

4.2   A review of the **purchasing accounting system** has resulted in the following recommendations:

4.2.1   The use of cheques to pay suppliers should be stopped and all paid by BACS. This will be more efficient and reduce the risk of manual errors and fraud. BACS will also be quicker and easier to countersign.

4.3   A review of **fraud controls** in place within the purchase accounting system has led to the following recommendations:

4.3.1   The payment of suppliers via BACS will reduce the risk of cheques being stolen. If not implemented it is recommended that cheques be kept in a safe locked cabinet and a log of all cheques kept.

4.3.2   The Accounts Manager should review financial health checks for new suppliers and approve them before contracts are signed. All new suppliers should only be set up once they have been approved by the Company Buyer and this should be checked by the Company Accountant.

4.3.3   DEL should appoint a senior manager to the role of Fraud Officer.

4.4   A review of **contingency planning** has resulted in the following recommendations:

4.4.1   DEL implement monthly meetings within the accounts team with a standing agenda including the discussion of key periods such as year end and that this is reviewed and discussed all year round.

4.4.2   Staff cover should be arranged for when staff are absent and DEL should consider recruiting temporary staff to cover longer term absence and have systems in place to re-distribute work accordingly.

4.4.3   DEL should invest in a back-up power system that generates more than 4 hours power per day, a procedure should be implemented during key busy periods to back the IT systems up twice daily and contingency plans need to be developed to cover the loss of system hardware.

4.4.4   Responsibility for updating systems and staff for regulation changes should be given to a key member of staff at senior level.

4.5   All these recommendations and the identification of weaknesses that led to them are discussed fully in the following report. A cost benefit analysis is included in appendix 6.

4.6   It is recommended that a review such as this is carried out 6 months after the implementation of these recommendations to ensure they are being implemented appropriately and that the improved cost effectiveness and efficiencies are being achieved.

4.7   It is then recommended that further review be carried out on an annual basis to ensure that the organisation continues to investigate its systems to ensure they are cost effective and efficient.

5 Management of People

5.1 The accounts team consists of 8 staff. The Company Accountant supervises and manages a team of 5 and reports to the Finance Director. There is an Accounting Technician who reports directly to the Finance Director. An organisation chart for the team is included in appendix 6.

5.2 The Finance Director is a qualified accountant who is responsible for the working capital of the organisation, produces the annual company report and statutory accounts and undertakes the role of Company Secretary.

5.3 The Company Accountant has full day-to-day responsibility for the running of the accounts department. They are AAT qualified and supervise the work of the accounting technicians and clerks. They are responsible for the production of the monthly management accounts and approve all payments made to suppliers.

5.4 The general ledger clerk is responsible for all data input into the general ledger and the monthly production of the trial balance. They also maintain the cash book and the petty cash. They are a trained personnel office and have no accounting qualifications.

5.5 The purchase ledger clerk is responsible for all data input and for the payment of suppliers. They also have experience in the sales ledger clerk's role and has completed the Foundation Level of the AAT qualification.

5.6 The sales ledger clerk and credit controller is responsible for all data input into the sales ledger and the credit control function. They have previous experience of working in a purchase ledger role and have no accounting qualifications.

5.7 The costing technician is responsible for costing the products DEL make. He has experience of working in a credit control role but no formal accounting qualifications.

5.8 The payroll and personnel clerk is responsible for the running of the monthly and weekly payroll and the maintenance of the personnel database. She has been extensively trained on the new payroll and personnel system but has no previous work experience or accounting qualifications.

5.9 The accounting technician reports to the Finance Director on systems and projects either for the Finance Director or the Company Accountant and is currently studying for the Technician Level of the AAT qualification. He has both sales and purchase ledger work experience.

5.10   Inductions:

5.10.1   There are no formal, planned inductions for new staff recruited to DEL although system related training is arranged for new staff if required.

5.11   Job Descriptions:

5.11.1   Job descriptions are not in place for staff.

5.12   Time Management:

5.12.1   Time management at DEL is poor. Little planning takes place for the financial year end which results in staff working long hours to complete all duties in the final few weeks of the year.

5.12.2   Lack of good time management is also evident in the role of the general ledger clerk who is extremely busy for one week of the month but then is not fully utilised the rest of the time.

5.12.3   Schedules exist for the planning of year end for both the sales and purchase ledger clerks with clear completion and cut-off dates.

5.12.4   The payroll clerk has clear deadlines for the completion of the payroll in time for the company year end of 31/03 and the tax year end of 05/04 although as these two deadlines are close this results in an extremely busy period.

5.12.5   Staff are able to take time off during very busy periods of the year.

5.13   Appraisals and Quality Controls:

5.13.1   All purchase invoices and payments to suppliers are approved by the Company Accountant prior to being processed.

5.13.2   No formal appraisals take place with staff and there are no other procedures in place to formally review their performance and the quality of their work.

5.14   Schedules & procedures:

5.14.1   Although some schedules exist for year end procedures they are being missed by staff as they are too busy during this period to work to them.

5.14.2   There are no formal procedures in place to explain how key tasks are completed.

5.15   Query Log:

5.15.1   A log of all queries passed to the accounting technician over a period of several weeks was kept and is included in this report as appendix 3.

5.15.2   Review of this log identifies that there are systems and procedures in place to make recommendations to improve processes or systems that are failing but that this is rather re-active and dependent on staff raising problems or complaints about the system they use.

5.16   Identification of Weaknesses:

5.16.1 The schedules in place for the sales and purchase ledger clerks at month end were not followed and so they completed their work late, this further impacted on the general ledger clerk who was unable to complete the trial balance until 2 weeks after their own deadline.

5.16.2 The general ledger clerk's working timetable will be de-motivating and is not well planned.

5.16.3 The deadline for the financial year end is 31/03 and this clashes with the payroll year end of 05/04 which results in an extremely busy period for the payroll clerk. The payroll clerk was unable to complete much of their work to the company deadlines due to this.

5.16.4 Staff are able to take annual leave during year end periods and this leads to additional pressure on the remaining staff. A lack of assistance from other members of the team will not promote a culture of team spirit and helping colleagues to complete deadlines.

5.16.5 Staff are not appraised and as a result the quality of their work is not reviewed and discussed. They are also not provided with a forum to discuss their own development and training needs and this could result in them becoming de-motivated. The lack of training will result in them being less efficient in the completion of their work and less able to support other team members during busy periods / absence.

5.16.6 The lack of company procedures for the completion of tasks is preventing staff assisting each other at busy periods or when staff are absent.

5.16.7 The lack of inductions may result in staff not feeling fully supported within their first few weeks at DEL and this could result in staff leaving or becoming de-motivated.

5.16.8 The lack of job descriptions leave staff feeling unsure as to what their role involves and could lead them being unwilling to complete additional tasks which they feel do not form part of their role within DEL. It could also result in difficulties with staff performance appraisal and quality control.

5.16.9 The lack of formal job descriptions, including key competencies required, may have resulted in DEL recruiting an inexperienced payroll clerk who had no prior knowledge of payroll systems or practices. This in turn has led to problems during key payroll periods and the new member of staff is unsupported in their role.

5.16.10 DEL do not conduct formal reviews of systems and processes on a regular basis to review their performance and suitability. This resulted in the failure of the payroll and personnel system to continue to meet DEL's requirements as it expanded not being identified until the payroll clerk was under a great deal of pressure and the system was failing to work effectively.

5.17 Recommendations:

5.17.1 The year end schedules and plans should be fully reviewed to ensure they are realistic and achievable and that where ever possible action is taken throughout the year to prepare so that staff do not miss the deadlines set. Staff should complete their own to-do lists and checklists for critical periods and be encouraged to make use of diaries and Outlook to assist them in planning their own time.

5.17.2 The work of the general ledger clerk should be reviewed so that either their work is spread evenly over the month or partnered with another clerk in the office so that they provide assistance when quiet and are given assistance when busy.

5.17.3 DEL should consider moving the financial year end to a period that does not clash with the payroll year end of 05/04. This will assist the Payroll clerk in their time management and enable more staff to assist them in the completion of the payroll year end.

5.17.4 DEL should consider a policy of not authorising annual leave during busy periods such as year end.

5.17.5 A formal system of staff appraisals should be implemented. The full appraisal should be conducted with staff once every 12 months and a follow-up one to one should take place every 3 months. Key targets should be set for performance and quality of work and training needs identified. Training should take place on a timely basis once the need has been identified.

5.17.6 A formal policy should be created for staff who wish to undertake training in accountancy qualifications and this should be encouraged. This will build a more motivated and knowledgeable accounts team.

5.17.7 A full procedures manual should be created for each role. Staff should be asked to document how they complete key tasks and this should be tested by asking staff to swap roles during quieter periods.

This will assist with them gaining a knowledge of each others' roles and responsibilities and also allow them to be able to cover when staff are absent or assist when staff are busy.

5.17.8 DEL should consider developing a formal induction programme for staff which includes appointing a senior member of staff as a mentor to help them through the first few months of employment. The induction should include formal training arranged when required but also feature an introduction to key staff, details of the company's background and history, and basic training on its systems and procedures. A formal follow-up to the induction should take place after a short period to ensure staff feel fully supported in their new role.

5.17.9 Formal job descriptions should be implemented for all staff including their key duties and responsibilities but also the need for them to complete additional tasks as required by the organisation. This would assist there is a need for them to be flexible and cover for absence or busy periods. The job descriptions should include key competencies required for staff in particular roles and would prevent recruiting unsuitable staff. They would also aid in staff appraisals and quality checks.

5.17.10 DEL should implement a review of systems and processes on a regular basis and it would be recommended that as DEL is expanding this be completed every 12 months. This would review their suitability for the business and ensure that potential problems are identified in advance and solutions considered and implemented before problems cause significant inefficiencies.

6 Purchase Accounting System

6.1 The purchases and supplier payments system is documented in a flow chart in appendix 1 and a SWOT in appendix 2.

6.2 DEL adopts a policy of partnership sourcing of suppliers and the company buyer is responsible for negotiating and agreeing 2-3 year contracts with suppliers with a annually negotiated price agreement.

6.3 New suppliers have financial checks completed by the purchase ledger clerk before contracts are signed.

6.4 When invoices and goods received notes are received they are sent to the company buyer to be checked and authorised before returning to the purchase ledger clerk for input to the purchase ledger system and posting to the general ledger.

6.5 Payments are made monthly through the production of a aged creditors list which identifies suppliers due for payment. They are authorised by the company accountant and one director.

6.6 Payments are made by cheque or BACS.

6.7 Weaknesses to the system:

6.7.1 The completion of cheques for some supplier payments is time consuming and the purchase ledger clerk is finding it increasingly difficult to ensure they are countersigned by one of the directors of the company.

6.7.2 The risk of errors in payments to suppliers is increased due to the completion of cheques. This then takes up additional time in double checking the correct completion of the cheques before they are signed.

6.7.3 The use of cheques also increases the risk of fraud which is discussed in more detail in Section 7.

6.8 Recommendations:

6.8.1 The use of cheques to pay suppliers should be stopped and all suppliers should be paid by BACS. This will be more efficient for DEL and also reduce the risk of manual errors and help prevent fraud. BACS will also be quicker and easier for the authorising signatories to approve.

7   Fraud Controls

7.1   The purchase ledger system is open to several possible frauds and some of these have been identified and analysed in the fraud matrix contained within appendix 5. If fraud were to take place the company would experience financial loss and the potential impact of such loss has been considered when grading the risk to the organisation. Fraud can be identified within the company by effective supervision of staff and by appropriate internal and external audits. The company does not currently have a senior manager designated as the fraud officer.

7.2   Identification of Weaknesses:

7.2.1   The risk of fraud is increased with the use of manual cheques for some payments to suppliers. Cheques could be stolen by staff and signatures copied. At present this risk is graded as high.

7.2.2   The use of cheques also opens DEL to the risk of collusion between the purchase ledger clerk and a supplier in overpayment of an account. The purchase ledger clerk could write a cheque for a larger amount than owed and without careful checks this could go unnoticed and be paid. This risk is graded as medium as the Company Accountant does check all payments before signing the cheques.

7.2.3   The purchase ledger system is also at risk of fraud through possible collusion between the clerk and a potential supplier when making financial checks before a new supplier is contracted with. It would be possible for the clerk to approve a new supplier whose financial health is poor as no formal appraisal is made by a more senior member of staff. This would be graded as medium risk.

7.2.4   The purchase ledger clerk also sets new suppliers up on the accounting system without further checks or controls as to whether they are approved. This could enable them to create a new dummy supplier with their own bank account details and pay them fraudulently through either a cheque payment or BACS.

7.2.5   The risk of fraud is increased by the lack of a senior manager designated as the company's Fraud Officer. This role is responsible for the investigation of potential frauds and controls in place plus acts as a contact for staff to report potential fraud that might be taking place.

7.3   Recommendations:

7.3.1   To prevent the risk of stolen cheques DEL could move to all suppliers being paid by BACS.

7.3.2   If this policy is not adopted it would be recommended that cheques be kept in a safe locked cabinet and a log of all cheques kept so that it could be identified if some were missing. It would also be recommended that an authorising signatory list be kept and that staff would not have access to the signatures contained on it.

7.3.3   The use of BACS would also reduce the risk of staff over-paying suppliers and this not being identified when checks are made.

7.3.4   It would be recommended that the purchase ledger clerk continues to prepare the financial health check information for new suppliers but that the Accounts Manager then checks this and approves the supplier before contracts are signed.

7.3.5   All new suppliers should only be set up on the purchase ledger system once they have been formally approved by the Company Buyer and this approval should be checked by the Company Accountant.

7.3.6   DEL should appoint a senior manager to the role of Fraud Officer.

8	**Contingency Planning**

8.1 Staff absence:

8.1.1 There is no formal system in place within DEL to cover staff's workloads when absent.

8.1.2 There are some staff with a working knowledge of other roles that their own but this is not recent and / or relevant to DEL.

8.1.3 This results in work becoming delayed and pressure on staff when they return to work.

8.1.4 Staff absence due to annual leave is not planned so that staff are able to take leave during the busiest periods of the year.

8.1.5 Staff have expressed that they are happy to cover absence through overtime but that this is not an option if it lasts any more than 2-3 working days.

8.1.6 No plans are in place to cover longer-term absence.

8.2 Loss of IT systems:

8.2.1 Plans are in place to cover the loss of systems due to a loss of power as a back-up generator is in place. This will provide up to 4 hours of power to DEL in any one working day.

8.2.2 The accounts team back-up the work completed on their systems daily, at the end of each working day so that if a failure in the system occurs a maximum of one day's work is lost and requires re-inputting to the systems.

8.2.3 There are no plans in place to cover long-term loss of power or loss of the IT hardware. This could occur for a variety of reasons such as fire, flood or theft.

8.3 Other changes to work patterns and demands:

8.3.1 DEL recently experienced a high workload within the accounts team due to the preparation of the final accounts at the company's year end. The Sales Ledger clerk was unable to complete their work appropriately due to their credit control responsibilities taking priority and this resulted in them working a 60-hour week to ensure their work was completed.

8.3.2 There was little support for the sales ledger clerk as other staff did not have the skills and experience required to assist them or were busy completing their own duties.

8.3.3 Due to both the sales and purchase ledger clerks missing deadlines the general ledger clerk was two weeks late in the production of the trial balance.

8.3.4   DEL do not have a policy in place for the introduction of new regulations that may affect how the accounting system operates such as a change in NIC contribution levels.

8.4   Identification of Weaknesses:

8.4.1   DEL has no formal review in place to identify possible peaks in the workload of staff and to plan for it appropriately. It is reliant on staff working long hours when required to ensure work is completed.

8.4.2   Staff are unable and / or unwilling to provide cover for each other when one is absent for any longer than a couple of days. This results in staff struggling to cope and key tasks left incomplete when staff are not there. This then impacts further on key deadlines such as month end and year end and results in additional overtime costs and poor staff morale.

8.4.3   There are no plans in place to cover long-term absence and it is expected that staff will cover this through working overtime. This approach would not be sustainable over an extended period as this would place too much pressure on staff working long hours. It does not also cover for when staff are absent during the busier periods when overtime is relied upon to complete routine work.

8.4.4   DEL's back-up power system only results in 4 hours of power being available per day. This is not an appropriate long-term solution to loss of power as it would result in lost production and administration time.

8.4.5   The back-up that takes place on the computer systems daily results in a maximum of one day's work being lost if the computer system fails but during busy periods this could be a significant amount of work lost that staff would struggle to repeat causing further delay and failure of deadlines.

8.4.6   DEL has no plans in place to recover the systems if hardware is lost, perhaps due to damage or theft. If this were to occur then this would result in a serious delay in recovery of work and systems which would impact on staff and the overall company.

8.4.7   The lack of a planned approach to changes in regulations such as the NIC contribution levels results in individual staff, who may lack the necessary training, knowledge or skills, being responsible for identifying and implementing such changes. This may result in some key regulation changes being missed which would mean statutory accounts or payroll would not be completed correctly.

8.5   Recommendations:

8.5.1   It is recommended that there be monthly meetings within the accounts team with a standing agenda including the discussion of key periods such as year end.

8.5.2   Staff cover should be arranged for when staff are absent through identifying key tasks that must be completed during the period and ensuring that staff are trained to do this. Less key tasks could then be left until staff return to work or, if the absence is long term, temporary staff could be recruited to cover these.

8.5.3   DEL should consider recruiting temporary staff to cover longer term absence and making use of the rescheduling of tasks recommended above.

8.5.4   DEL should consider investigating a back-up power system that generates more than 4 hours' power per day.

8.5.5   A procedure should be implemented during key busy periods to back the IT systems up twice daily, at lunch time and the end of the day. This will result in less work being lost and less staff time being spent re-entering lost work.

8.5.6   Contingency plans need to be developed to cover the loss of system hardware.   It is recommended that DEL investigate insurance schemes that provide replacement hardware within a maximum time period (eg 24 hours) if this is the case.

8.5.7   Responsibility for updating systems and staff for regulation changes should be given to a key member of staff at senior level such as the Finance Director. This would reduce the risk of changes not being identified and implemented by inexperienced staff.

9   **Appendices**

APPENDIX 1

Flow chart of the Purchases and Supplier Payments System

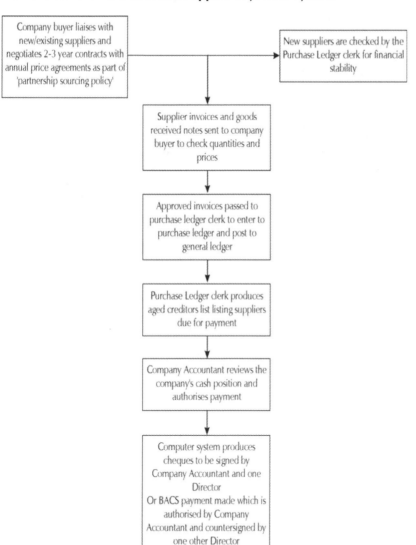

Company buyer liaises with new/existing suppliers and negotiates 2-3 year contracts with annual price agreements as part of 'partnership sourcing policy'

New suppliers are checked by the Purchase Ledger clerk for financial stability

Supplier invoices and goods received notes sent to company buyer to check quantities and prices

Approved invoices passed to purchase ledger clerk to enter to purchase ledger and post to general ledger

Purchase Ledger clerk produces aged creditors list listing suppliers due for payment

Company Accountant reviews the company's cash position and authorises payment

Computer system produces cheques to be signed by Company Accountant and one Director
Or BACS payment made which is authorised by Company Accountant and countersigned by one other Director

APPENDIX 2

SWOT

Strengths:	Weaknesses:
2-3 year contracts through partnership sourcing of suppliers Financial checks of new suppliers Invoices checked and authorised Payments made monthly Payments authorised	Cheque payments – errors / fraud / stolen cheques / authorisation PL could approve poor new supplier Possible to overpay an account No Fraud Officer
Opportunities:	**Threats:**
Other staff in the department have sales and purchase ledger experience BACS	Outsourcing of these types of accountancy roles popular Suppliers might resist BACS

APPENDIX 3

Query Log

Query	How Resolved	Who referred to/why
Report of very slow payroll system from Payroll clerk	Payroll clerk asked to monitor and keep records of when system is slow to enable picture to be developed of when problems occur	
Payroll clerk reports that system is experiencing increased problems and getting slower and or crashes frequently – records as requested provided	Accounting technician sat with payroll clerk to gain further understanding of problems with system	Referred to Finance Director through written report of problems with recommendation that new integrated payroll and personnel package be implemented

APPENDIX 4

Summary results from staff interviews:

What is your Job Title?	Do you have a formal qualification?	What are you resposible for?	What other experience do you have?
Finance Director	Qualified accountant	Working capital Annual Co Report Statutory Accounts Company Secretary	
Company Accountant	AAT Qualified	Surpervise technicians clerks Production of monthly management accounts Approve payments to suppliers	
GL Clerk	NO – but trained personnel officer	Maintain Cash book and petty cash Data input to GL Production of trial balance	Personnel
PL Clerk	Foundation level of AAT	Data input Payments to suppliers	Sales Ledger
SL Clerk	No	Input to sales ledger Credit control	Purchase Ledger
Costing technician	No	Costing DEL products	None
Payroll and Personnel Clerk	No	Running monthly payroll Running weekly payroll Maintenance of personnel database	None
Accounting Technician	Study Technician level of AAT	Reports to Finance Director – systems and projects	Sales & purchase ledger

APPENDIX 5

Fraud Matrix:

Potential fraud	Control in place	Risk to DEL	Recommendation
Stolen cheques	None	4	BACS or lock cheques away
Company Accountant	Company Accountant checks all payments	3	BACS/careful checks
Collusion with new supllier	Financial checks	3	Senior staff approve new suppliers
PL Clerk puts new suppliers on the system	No checks that supplier is approved	4	Checks by Company Accountant
No Fraud Officer	None	4	Appoint Fraud Officer

Key to grading – 1 = low risk, 5 = high risk

APPENDIX 6

Recommendation	Cost	Benefit
Review year end schedules and plans	½ day – Accountant	Deadlines are met and year end completed on time
Review work of general ledger clerk	1 day – Accountant & GL clerk	Improved planning and motivation
Implement staff appraisals and training plans	1 day to set up and time to complete appraisals and follow ups	Motivated staff, targets achieved, better training
Create procedure manual	2-3 days for each member of staff	Improved cover and better planning / work
Implement BACS payments	Cost of BACS system	Less risk / better control
Appoint senior manager as Fraud Officer	Pay increase 2 days per month on duties	Reduced risk of fraud / better controls
Implement monthly meetings	2 hours per month – all staff	Better planning / control
Recruit temp staff to cover absence	Hourly cost of staff	Improved cover
Better back up power system	£10,000	Less downtime if power lost
Hardware insurance	£350 pa	Less cost to replace hardware and improved recovery time

APPENDIX 7

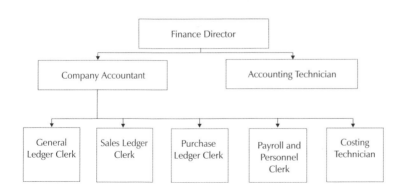

student notes

INDEX